CREATIVE WAYS with

Books and Journals

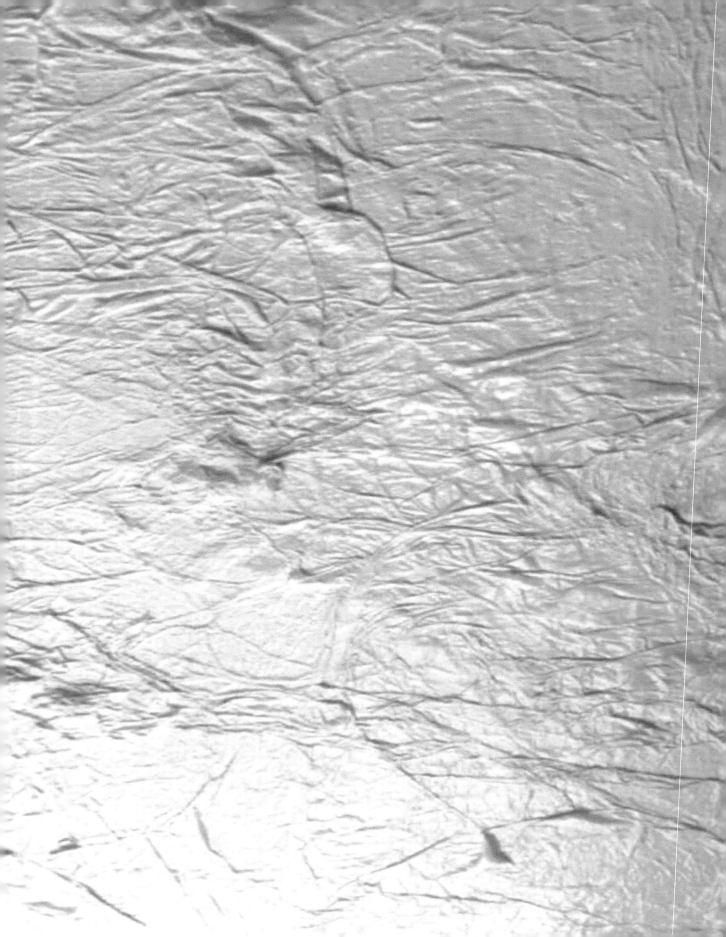

CREATIVE WAYS

with

Books and Journals

Sue Bleiweiss & Terri Stegmiller

Table of Contents

6

Introduction

Are you one of those people who has a pile of blank books and journals that you just can't bring yourself to write in? If you are, you're not alone. Most of us, at one time or another, have come home from the store with a blank book we fell in love with and just had to have. You stand there in the store, holding the book in your hand, imagining all the wonderful things you'll write or draw in it. And then you got home with your new book and all those crisp, clean, blank pages that seemed so ripe with possibilities in the store suddenly look too blank and white and boring to inspire you to do anything with them. So you put the book on the shelf where it sits unused with all the other blank books whose white pages overwhelm you every time you look at them.

Now imagine you're holding a book you've made yourself, that's filled with no scary, blank, white pages. A book that you made yourself from scratch, that when opened is filled with colorful pages that you've painted yourself. Each page a colorful canvas just waiting for you to doodle, collage, draw or sketch on. Suddenly a door of possibilities opens for you because there's no blank page to be intimidated by.

Once you've experienced the pleasure of creating your own books and journals from scratch you'll find that you'll be much more motivated to use them. There is a special feeling that you get when you hold a book you've made yourself in your hand; and even if the only thing you write in your book is your to-do list, you'll find that there is no substitute for the satisfaction of knowing that you're writing in a book you made with your own two hands.

In the pages of this book you'll find twelve unique and creative books to get you started on your book making journey—each with a surface design technique to make the outsides of your book just as interesting as the inside. We encourage you to start by reading through the tools & materials, colored backgrounds and making and sewing signatures sections before you begin making any of the books. Each of these sections contains a wealth of helpful information that will make it easy for you to complete the book projects successfully.

A favorite quote by Charles W. Eliot tells us that:

> Books are the quietest and most constant of friends; they are the most accessible and wisest of counselors, and the most patient of teachers.

So make yourself a new friend to write, doodle, sketch or draw in! You'll be glad you did.

Sue Bleiweiss & Terri Stegmiller

CHAPTER 1

Tools & Materials

Tools & Materials

All of the books and journals in this book are made with easy-to-find supplies and most can be purchased from local craft and fabric stores. In some cases we've included names of our favorite brands, but you should always feel free to work with your own favorites and we encourage you to experiment with new ones as well.

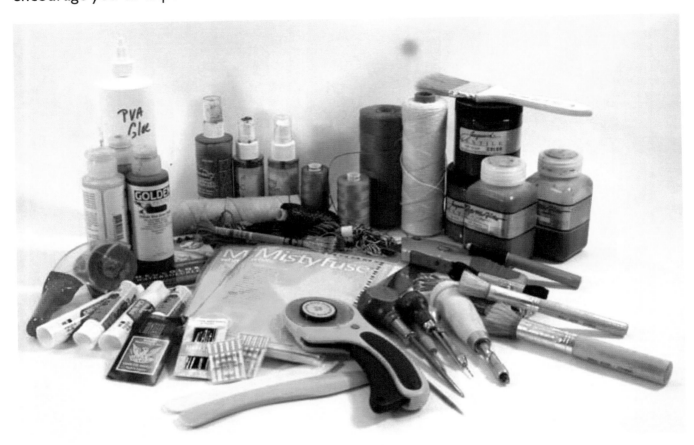

Fusible web

There are a lot of fusible web products on the market but our preferred fusible web is Mistyfuse. This is a paperless, very lightweight fusible that fuses sheer when you use a piece of Reynolds parchment paper as the press cloth. A Teflon pressing sheet will create a shiny surface. We use this fusible because we can always count on getting a good, strong bond and when used for foiling on the surface it doesn't leave a shiny surface residue that other fusibles leave behind. It works great on both paper and fabric.

Glue

There are a lot of different types of glues available to the crafter these days. For book making we prefer to use PVA glue available from most book binding supply stores. When working with thin papers, where liquid glue may cause the paper to become too fragile and cause tearing, a glue stick is a great alternative to liquid PVA glue. Make sure that the glue stick you choose says "permanent" on the label. Otherwise you may find that your glued surfaces separate after a period of time.

You can buy expensive glue brushes, for spreading PVA glue onto surfaces, from most bookbinding suppliers, but inexpensive stencil brushes or chip brushes work just as nicely.

Interfacing and stabilizers

These come in a wide variety of weights and types and it's important to choose the right one for the project that you're working on. Interfacings come in both fusible and non-fusible types, as well as woven and non-woven, and are typically used to add strength and stability to fabrics.

When we refer to stabilizers in this book we are referring to products that add not only stiffness but also add body to our projects. There are several options to choose from when picking a stabilizer so use this as general guide:

Timtex: the stiffest of all the stabilizers. This product is especially helpful when creating 3-D structures such as boxes and vases.

Fast2Fuse: This is a similar product to Timtex but it has a fusible web applied to both sides.

Pellon Peltex #70: A lighter weight stabilizer. This is our preferred stabilizer for making fabric and soft covered journals. It has just the right amount of stiffness without adding too much bulk. It's also available with pre-applied fusible web on one side (Peltex #71) or on both sides (Peltex #72).

Pelmet Vilene: Another lighter weight stabilizer, similar to Pellon Peltex.

Stiffy: This is a very inexpensive product similar in weight to Pelmet Vilene and Pellon Peltex.

There are many more of these products on the market. Experiment to find the ones that you like working with.

Book board

For making hard cover books there's no substitute for book board (also known as binders board). Book board comes in a variety of weights but we prefer working with the .087 board available from Hollander's (see Resources).

Paints, crayons and oil sticks

There are a lot of paints, crayons, markers and oil sticks on the market to choose from. Use the brands you favor and know will give you the results you want. It pays to experiment with different brands and types to determine which are the ones that give you the results that you want. Don't be afraid to use a paint on paper that's made for fabric, you may be pleasantly surprised at the result you get.

Sewing tools

Some of the projects in this book require the use of a sewing machine. Always keep your machine clean and free of dust and debris. Make sure you're using a good, sharp needle in the appropriate size for the project you're making. A worn and dull needle will cause thread breaks and other headaches, so it's important to change the needle regularly especially if you do a lot of mixed-media sewing, such as sewing on paper, foils and other non-traditional surfaces.

Sewing on paper doesn't require any special tools or threads but you do want to increase your stitch length a bit to avoid perforating the paper.

When sewing by hand use a strong, sharp needle. In most cases you may find it helpful to pre-punch your sewing holes to make it easier on your hands.

Cutting tools

Keep your scissors and your rotary cutter blades sharp and clean and they'll be easier and smoother to cut with. If you have to use a lot of pressure and find yourself struggling to push the rotary cutter through the fabric, chances are the blade is dull and needs to be changed.

When cutting book board you'll need to use a heavy duty straight-edged cutter with a new, sharp blade. A sharp blade is essential! You'll find that cutting book board dulls your blades pretty quickly so you'll want to have a good supply on hand.

Along with a utility knife you'll need to have a metal edge ruler. Do NOT try to use a utility knife with a clear plastic quilting ruler! You'll ruin the ruler. Check your local office supply store for metal rulers or you can get them from an online supplier.

Paper

Of course you'll want to have some decorative paper for your journals and books. You'll find a wide variety of papers available from the book binding resources listed in the back of this book. Wrapping paper, scrapbook paper and old maps and other papers will also work.

For the inside text pages of your books and journals you can use any type of paper you like. Take a trip to the office supply store and you'll find that copy and printer paper is easily and readily available and comes in a variety of weights and colors. You can also use drawing, sketch or watercolor paper.

Book cloth

This is essentially starched fabric that has been bonded with a paper backing (some don't have a paper backing). Using book cloth for the spines of your hardcover books gives it a professional look and creates a sturdy hinge for the covers that won't tear when your book is opened. You can easily make your own book cloth by using Mistyfuse to fuse a layer of tissue paper to the back of your well-pressed, wrinkle-free fabric.

Linen or cotton threads

You'll want to have a selection of threads to sew your pages into your journals. You can use linen book binders thread, cotton floss or any sturdy thread or twine you have on hand. An easy way to determine if the thread you want to use is strong enough, is to tug on it. If it snaps or breaks apart easily then it's probably not sturdy enough to use to sew in your pages.

Awls

The safest and easiest way to poke holes in the spines of your books is to use an awl. They come in a variety of sizes and shapes and you'll need to experiment with different types to find the one that works best for you. You can also use a small hand drill or Japanese screw punch to make the holes in your book surfaces.

Bone folders

Using a bone folder to set the creases in your folded pages will give you a crisp result. They come in a variety of shapes, sizes and materials including bone, plastic and Teflon.

Closures

There are a lot of options available for adding closures to your books and journals. You can wrap your book with a piece of ribbon or yarn to keep it closed.

Some other ideas:

Elastic cord or braid—Tie a button to the front of your book using twine or thread. Feed a small piece of elastic cord through an eyelet installed on the back cover, knot the end to prevent it from slipping through the hole and then pull the loop around the button. Or you can punch a hole in the center of the spine of the book, fold a length of elastic cord in half and then pull the loop end through the hole from the inside to the outside. A knot on the inside will keep the elastic from slipping through.

Suede or leather cord—Look for these cords in the jewelry making aisle in the craft shop. You can usually get them in a wide variety of colors and textures.

Leather closures—Look for these in the scrapbook supply store. Two brands that we like are Zutter and Teresa Collins. You can paint these leather straps, to match the theme of your book, using textile paints. They're very easy to install and the directions are on the back of the package.

CHAPTER 2

Colored Backgrounds

Colored Backgrounds

You'll find yourself more inspired to write in the books and journals that you create if you take the time to make the inside pages colorful and exciting. After all, a page that is washed with color is much easier to jump in and start writing or drawing on than starting with a plain white page. You could, of course, add color to your pages after your journal is all assembled but you may find the process much more fun if you prepare your painted papers in advance. Remember that as you're creating colored papers for your journals that it's not essential to completely cover the entire page with color. At some point you might want to use these pages to journal or sketch on, so some white spaces are okay. You can use those white spaces as ways to highlight some text or frame a sketch or doodle on the page later on.

Here are some easy methods for creating colorful painted background papers for your journals.

Glass printing

Be aware that this process is addictive! You can get some wonderful effects using this technique and it's by far one of our favorites. You can use any paint you like for this technique. Acrylic craft and textile paints both work very well.

You can use a piece of plexi-glass or plastic in place of the glass, if you prefer. If you're working with glass, tape the edges to avoid cutting yourself. Handle the glass carefully so as not to break or damage it. You could even do this technique on some cardboard wrapped in plastic or on a piece of freezer paper if you don't have access to a piece of glass or plexi-glass.

Start by choosing two or three colors of paint that work well together. This will allow you to move from one color to the next without having to clean the glass. Choose one of the colors to start with and drop some of it and some white paint onto the surface of the glass.

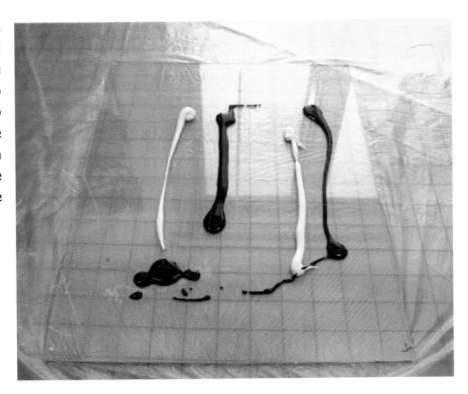

Use a foam brush to spread the paint out a bit.

Place your paper over the paint and use a brayer to roll across the surface to make sure that the paper comes in contact with the paint. If you don't have a brayer then an old rolling pin wrapped in plastic will work too.

Brayer from the center out. This pushes some of that excess paint out to the edges where it will transfer to the brayer and as you roll the brayer back and forth along the paper you'll add color to the back side of the paper as well.

When you're done, carefully peel back the paper and set it aside to dry.

Depending on how much paint you dropped onto the surface to start, there's probably a good amount still left on the glass. You can probably get at least a couple more pieces of paper painted without adding any more paint to the surface. Simply repeat the brayering process that you used with the first sheet.

Once you've exhausted the paint that's on the glass, go ahead and add your second color along with some more white paint. As long as you've chosen a color that blends well with the first color, you'll get a great result. The original color that remains on the glass will blend with the new color, creating a beautiful piece of paper.

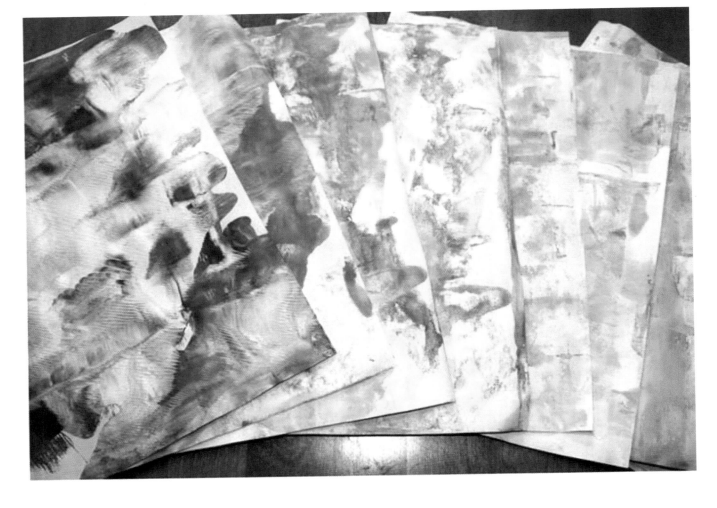

Other easy and fun ways to add color and interest to your papers:

Spray it on!

Liquid watercolors and spray inks are a fast and easy way to add color to paper. The liquid watercolors (Dick Blick makes a great one, see Resources) are watercolor paints in liquid form and they can be transferred to a spray bottle to make them easier to use. You can also dilute them with water for softer colors.

Spray your paper with some of the watercolors or inks and while the paint is wet add a layer of crumpled plastic wrap right on top. Let it sit for a few minutes and then pull the plastic off. Another option is to spray the color on and then use a piece of plastic wrap to pounce across the surface.

Spray your paper with the color and then use a piece of paper towel to move the paint across the surface. The more you brush the surface the more color you'll pull off and the more blending you'll get.

Place a piece of rug canvas on your paper and then spray over it with paint. Lift off the rug canvas and you're left with a wonderful pattern on the surface of the paper. Try this with other things—paper clips, washers, coins, doilies etc.

As your painted papers dry they will curl. When they are completely dry, press them with a hot iron under a piece of parchment paper to flatten them out.

Rubber stamp pads
Drag a rubber stamp pad across the surface of your paper to add color.

Coffee & tea
Stain your papers with cold brewed coffee or tea for a vintage look.

Water-soluble crayons
Scribble on your paper with a water-soluble crayon and then spritz it with water. Blend the colors together with a piece of paper toweling or a paint brush.

Colored pencils, markers and pens
Add some doodles and scribbles along the margins of your papers to create borders around the page. Use gel pens to add a little shimmer.

Leftover dye
If you dye your own fabrics, use any leftovers after a dye session to color your paper.

Faux marbling
Spray a layer of white foamy shave cream into a tray. Drip some thin paint (Jacquard Dye-Na-Flow works perfectly for this) onto the surface. Use a skewer, knife or old comb to swirl the paint through the shave cream. Lay your paper on top, press it to the surface to remove any air bubbles, lift it off and scrape off the excess shave cream from surface.

CHAPTER 3

Making & Sewing Signatures

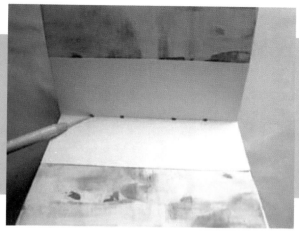

Making & Sewing Signatures

A signature is a fancy name for the inside pages of a book and you can make your books and journals with as many signatures as you want.

Choosing the paper

The first thing you'll need to do is choose your paper for your signatures. You can use any type of paper for this. Take a trip to the office supply store and you'll find that copy and printer paper is easily and readily available and comes in a variety of weights and colors. Drawing, sketch and watercolor paper are all good choices as well. Choose your paper based on what you will use your journal for. If you know that you will be using a lot of wet media such as watercolors or paints, then make sure you choose a paper that won't deteriorate when it gets wet.

Once you have chosen the type of paper you want to fill your journal with you'll need to cut it to size. As a general rule it's a good idea to cut your paper ½" smaller that the height of your journal. So if your journal height is 9" then your paper should be 8½" high. This insures that the paper won't peek out over the edges and saves the edges from any wear and tear if the journal is stored upright.

The width of your paper is determined by the width of your journal. Always test a folded piece of the paper size you intend to use before preparing the entire signature to make sure that it will fit in your journal shell without hanging over the edge.

Remember that the pages in your signatures do not all have to be the same size and color!

The signature in this book was made from a combination of painted watercolor, drawing and sketch paper in a variety of sizes. When it comes to the paper you use to make your signatures, your only limit is your own imagination.

Once you have your pieces of paper cut to size, fold them in half to make your signature pages. Avoid trying to fold too many pieces together at once. This makes for a messy and uneven fold.

Depending on the thickness of the paper that you're using you may want to fold each page individually. After you have folded them all, divide them into even piles of three (or however many signatures your book will have) and then nest the pages together to form a signature.

Some other ideas for paper sources for your signatures might be:

Unprinted newsprint – visit your local newspaper office to see if they sell end rolls. Most do at very reasonable prices.

Raid the recycle bin!

Use colored catalog or magazine pages – coat them with a layer of gesso and then write and collage right over them.

Old notebooks – everybody usually has some old notebooks lying around that are either half filled or unused. Tear out the pages and use them for paper in your hand made journals.

Getting ready to sew your signatures into your journal

Now that you've created your signatures you need to sew them into your journal. Before you can do this you'll need to determine how many and where to punch your sewing holes in both the signature and the journal shell itself.

Four-hole stitch pattern

To create a four-hole punch guide for your signatures take a piece of paper the same size as your signature pages and fold it in half. Using a ruler and a sharp pencil make four marks in the fold of the page starting from the top at: 1½" from the top, then 3" from the top, 5½" from the top and 7" from the top.

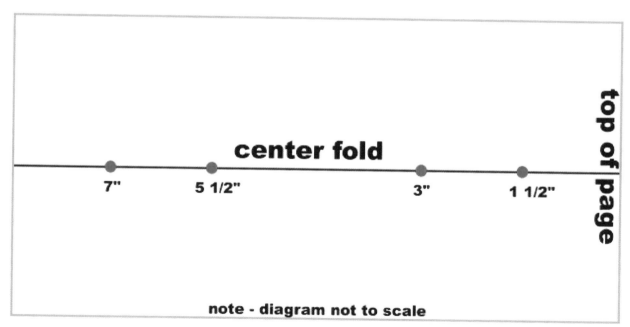

These measurements assume that you're using a piece of paper that is 8½" high. If you're using a smaller piece of paper then you'll need to adjust the hole placement accordingly.

Place your hole-punching guide in the center of one of your signatures aligning the top and bottom edges and use a sharp awl to poke a hole, where your marks are, all the way through the entire signature.

BE CAREFUL not to poke yourself with the awl! Do this for all of your signatures and then set them aside while you punch the corresponding holes in the actual journal spine.

Tip: It's important that your holes are exactly in the fold of the signature, otherwise you may have problems sewing your signatures into your book. To make this easier you can purchase a hole-punching cradle.

These cradles come in many different sizes and materials such as book board, metal and wood. The one you see here is a smaller metal version that's perfect for taking to classes. To use it, just place your signature in the cradle and then use your awl to punch through holes in the guide.

Now you can make a hole-punching guide for the spine of your journal. Cut a piece of book board or cardboard the same width as the spine piece of your book and the same height of your journal, which is typically ½" taller than the signatures. Mark a line ¼" from the top edge and then from the bottom edge. The space between is where your holes should be placed. This insures that your signatures won't end up too close to the top or bottom edges of the journal. Use a ruler and a sharp pencil to make four marks along the center of the guide starting from the top 1/4" line that you marked at: 1½" from the line, then 3" from the line, 5½" from the line and 7" from the line.

After you mark the holes in the center column then mark the outer column of holes on both sides ¼" away from the center holes. If you are making more than three signatures for your book, space the columns of holes evenly across the width of the template, keeping the outermost holes ¼" away from each outer edge of the template.

The very center single hole in this template is used when you want to mark a hole that can be used to thread an elastic closure through, so it is optional. With the journal inside facing up on your work surface you can place the spine hole-punching guide on top of the book spine. Mark the holes in the spine and then use a sharp awl to punch through them.

Sewing in your signatures

Now that your holes are all punched you can sew in your signatures. You can use linen book binders thread, cotton floss or any sturdy thread or twine you have on hand. An easy way to determine if the thread you want to use is strong enough is to tug on it, if it snaps or breaks apart easily then it's probably not sturdy enough to use to sew in your pages.

You can also use ribbon, torn pieces of fabric and even novelty yarns to sew in your signatures. You may need to make your holes bigger to accommodate these, so keep that in mind when making your choice.

To sew your signatures into your journal using a four-hole pattern, thread a tapestry needle with a length of embroidery floss or linen twine that is at least twice as long as the height of your book. You can use either a single or doubled length of thread.

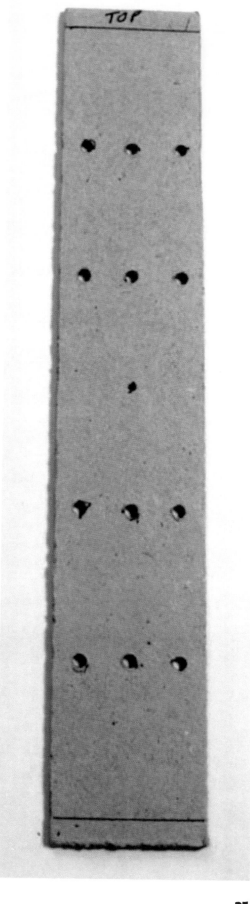

Line one signature up with one set of holes and starting from the inside sew through the second hole from the top of the signature to the outside of the journal through the corresponding hole in the journal shell, leaving a 6" tail on the inside.

Then sew through the top outside hole of the journal shell and through the inside top hole of the signature.

Sew through the bottom hole of the signature and out through the bottom hole of the journal shell.

Sew back through the third hole from the top of the journal shell and back through the inside corresponding hole of the signature.

Tie off the thread using the tail that you left hanging. It's a good idea to tie a double knot and then put a dab of Fray Check or glue on the knot to make sure that it will not come untied. Repeat this entire process to sew the other signatures into the book.

Three-hole stitch pattern

Here's an alternative way to sew in your signatures. You'll need to prepare a hole-punching guide that has three holes in it. Place the middle hole in the center of the page and then the other two will be placed ½" to 1" away from the top and bottom edge of the page depending on the size of the paper that you're using.

To sew your signature into your journal begin by stitching through the center hole to the outside leaving a tail of 6" on the inside. Sew through the top hole back to the inside of the signature and then sew out through the bottom hole of the signature to the outside of the journal. Sew through the center hole back to the inside and tie off using the tail you left hanging.

Tip: If you want your thread tails to end up on the outside of your journal then start sewing from the outside. Thread some beads onto the tails when you're finished sewing as a nice decorative touch to your journal.

Two-hole stitch pattern

For smaller books you can use a two-hole stitch pattern. This book stands only 5" high and beads were added during the stitching step to add an additional decorative element to the spine.

CHAPTER 4

Painted Fabric Journals

Silk Shibori Journal

Create a gorgeous silk journal using an easy Shibori technique known as Arashi or pole-wrapping Shibori. This method of dyeing or painting fabric creates a wonderfully unique and beautiful piece of cloth. This technique creates a stunning piece of fabric when used with silk but it also works just as nicely with cotton, linen or even silk velvet.

SUPPLIES NEEDED

For painting the silk:
- 100% Habotai silk
- 1½" diameter PVC pipe
- Jacquard Dye-Na-Flow
- String, twine, or cotton thread

For making the journal:
- ½ yard of painted silk
- Lightweight fusible interfacing (optional)
- Peltex
- Mistyfuse
- Parchment paper
- 1½" button cover kit
- Cord or ribbon
- Paper for the inside pages of the journal

STEP 1: Cut a two-yard length of the Habotai silk. Then cut it in half the long way, making a 72" x 22½" piece of cloth.

Wet your piece of fabric and then wring out the excess water. The silk should be wet but not dripping with water.

STEP 2: Wrap the wet silk fabric around the PVC pipe starting at one end.

Continue wrapping the silk around the pipe until all the fabric is on the pipe. Don't worry about the fabric folding up onto itself while wrapping. These folds will act as additional resists for the paint, resulting in a more complex looking piece of cloth. When all of the silk has been wrapped onto the pole, stand the pole up and push the fabric down to scrunch it together a bit.

STEP 3: Secure the fabric to the pole. Wrap some twine or cotton thread around it.

STEP 4: Add some color! Jacquard Dye-Na-Flow paints are a favorite with this technique. Other silk paints or dyes may be substituted. Decant the paint into squeeze bottles (that are clearly marked with the color name and number) to make the paint application easier.

Saturate the wet silk with color. You can use one or several colors. If you work with several colors, choose ones that play well together, since the paints will run together as the fabric dries. It's important to make sure that you use enough paint to completely saturate the fabric otherwise you may end up with unpainted areas.

Tip: If you are working directly out of the paint jars, decant some of the paint into a small bowl and use a foam brush that's been dampened with water. Dip the brush into the paint and then squish it into the fabric to push the paint into the folds.

Once you have completely saturated the cloth with paint, stand the pipe up in a tray that has been covered with plastic to catch the paint that drips off the fabric while it dries. Alternatively, you can leave the pipe laying on it's side. If you leave it to dry while it's horizontal, put something under the ends to lift it off the surface a bit so that the fabric is not resting on the tray.

It can take anywhere from several days up to a week for the fabric to completely dry. After a day of drying, all of the excess paint will have collected in the tray and you can use this to paint another piece of fabric. Carefully move the pipe to another tray and then place a piece

of wet silk into the tray and press it into the paint. Leave it in the paint to dry or take it out and leave it to dry in a crumpled heap on another piece of plastic. You'll end up with another beautiful piece of cloth.

STEP 5: Once your fabric has completely dried on the pipe, unwrap it and heat set it according to the manufacturer's directions for the paint that you have used. To heat set the fabrics that are painted with Dye-Na-Flow paint, steam press the fabric first to iron out the wrinkles and then put it in the clothes dryer for 30 minutes on high heat. At this point the color should be set and the silk can be washed in a washing machine on the gentle cycle and dried in the dryer.

STEP 6: Make the journal.

Before you begin, press your silk fabric well to iron out any wrinkles. When working with the silk it is helpful to fuse a lightweight fusible interfacing to the back side of the fabric. This is an optional step but it makes the silk easier to handle while assembling the journal.

Cut a piece of Peltex and two pieces of Mistyfuse that measure 9" x 18" Using parchment paper to protect your iron and ironing surface, press with a hot iron to fuse one piece of Mistyfuse to one side of the Peltex. Let cool and remove the parchment paper.

Cut two pieces of silk to cover both sides of the Peltex. It is much easier to cut your silk slightly larger than your Peltex. This will insure that all of the Peltex will be covered with the silk. Place a piece of silk over the Peltex that has Mistyfuse adhered to it. Cover with parchment paper and press with your iron to fuse the silk to the Peltex. Let cool, remove the parchment paper and trim off the excess silk that extends beyond the Peltex edges. Repeat on the other side of the Peltex with the other piece of Mistyfuse and silk.

STEP 7: Choose one side of your silk-covered Peltex to be the lining or inside of the journal.

If you would like your journal to have a decorative edge on the flap then place the cover with the lining side facing up and cut a wavy edge along the right side.

To add a pocket to the inside front of the journal, cut a piece of fabric 9" x 8". Fold it in half to make a piece of fabric 9" x 4" and press it well. With the journal lining side up, place the pocket piece along the left edge aligning the raw edges of the pocket with the edge of the journal. You can pin it in place to keep it from shifting while you finish the edges of the journal.

Set your sewing machine for a wide zigzag stitch (or a satin stitch if you prefer) and stitch all around the edges of the journal, taking care to catch the edges of the pocket in the stitching.

Tip: When satin stitching the edges of journals, use a zigzag stitch set very wide, but not too dense, and stitch around twice instead of once. You will find that using two layers of thinner stitching gives a better result than trying to get total coverage with one layer of stitching.

STEP 8: Prepare three signatures for the inside of your journal using paper measuring 8½" x 11" and folded in half to make pages 5½" x 8½". Using a four-hole punching guide as described in *Making and Sewing Signatures* beginning on page 21, punch the holes in your signatures.

Open up the journal cover and with the lining side up, place your hole-punching guide about 6½" in from the left edge and punch the holes in the journal cover.

Thread a tapestry needle with an 18" length of embroidery floss, linen twine or other sturdy thread and sew in the signatures following the four-hole stitching pattern on page 26.

STEP 9: Add a button to the outside of your journal by using a button cover kit to create a coordinating button. Or, if you prefer, you can use a purchased button.

Cut a length of ribbon or cording to wrap around your journal to keep it closed. Cut the ribbon long enough to go around the journal twice. Tie one end around the button and then wrap it around the journal.

Signatures

Quilted & Painted Journal

Quilting adds so much dimension and texture to quilts so why not use the same technique for your journal cover? Quilt your design free-motion style first, and then paint it in your favorite colors. This journal is created in three pieces to mimic the look of a hard cover book.

SUPPLIES NEEDED

Light-colored fabric
Low-loft quilt batting
Stiffy interfacing
Fabric to line the inside of your journal
Mistyfuse
Parchment paper
Water-erasable pen
Ruler
Water-soluble crayons
Gesso
Paintbrushes
Textile medium
Paper for the inside pages of the journal

STEP 1: Cut the light-colored fabric, Stiffy, quilt batting, lining fabric and three pieces of Mistyfuse to 10½" x 16". Set aside the lining fabric and one piece of Mistyfuse for later.

STEP 2: Create a sandwich on your ironing surface starting with a sheet of parchment paper. Place the layers on top of the parchment paper, starting with the Stiffy, as shown in the diagram. Place a sheet of parchment paper on the top over the light-colored fabric.

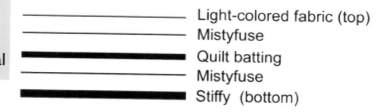

— Light-colored fabric (top)
— Mistyfuse
— Quilt batting
— Mistyfuse
— Stiffy (bottom)

Press with a hot iron to fuse all the layers together. Because the unit is thick with many layers, you will need to use steam or hold the iron in place a bit longer for the heat to penetrate. Once you have pressed the top side well, flip the entire unit over, parchment paper included, and heat from the opposite side to ensure a good bond.

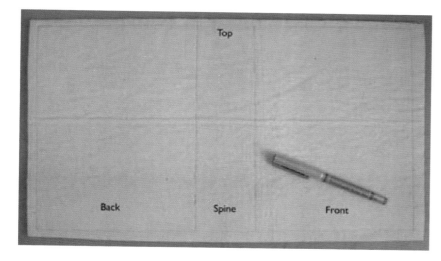

Top

Back   Spine   Front

STEP 3: Using the ruler and water-erasable marking pen (or light pencil marks), mark the outer edge borders of the front, back, and spine pieces.

Draw a rectangle measuring 9½" x 15". Then add a vertical line 6½" from the line on the left side and 6½" from the line on the right side. These are border guidelines for the front, back and spine. You will fill these areas in with your quilting. They are oversized and will be trimmed later. Plan your quilting design accordingly to fit within the space. It can be helpful to mark which area is the back, spine, front and top to keep your quilting design oriented in the right direction.

Tip: Stiffy interfacing is used in this project, because it is a thinner interfacing than Timtex or Peltex. Because this project has the added batting layer, the Stiffy interfacing is the perfect choice.

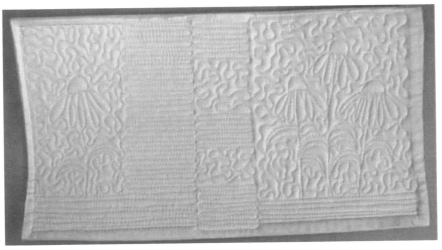

STEP 4: Using a matching thread, machine quilt your design. The quilting can be executed in a free-motion style or using a machine-guided stitch. You may find it helpful to draw your planned design onto your fabric—use the water-eraseable pen or light pencil lines. Fill the entire area of all three sections with stitching.

STEP 5: Lightly spray water onto the water-eraseable pen marks to make them disappear. You can also dampen a rag and blot the lines away. Let dry.

STEP 6: (optional) With a 1" to 2" paintbrush, lightly brush gesso randomly over the surface of the fabric. Dip the brush into the gesso and work some of the gesso off the brush onto your palette, so you aren't applying a thick layer.

You don't want to brush it into the stitched areas of the fabric, just across the raised areas. The gesso should be applied randomly and not over the entire surface. It is used to add textural interest and will act, somewhat as a resist when you paint. Opaque white acrylic paint can be substituted for the gesso. Let it dry thoroughly.

STEP 7: Use the water-soluble crayons to add color to your design. Note that transparent acrylic paint may be substituted for water-soluble crayons. When applying the color to the fabric with the crayon, you don't need to color the area

in fully and you don't need to color all the way to the outer stitching lines. When you have an area colored dip your paintbrush into the textile medium and start brushing it over the colored fabric. The color will become wet and will spread around to an extent. If you would like to deepen the color, dip your paintbrush in the medium and brush the tip of the crayon with it to pick up more color on the brush and then paint it onto the fabric. Add color to all areas of your quilted surface remembering to add dark color and white for shading and highlights. When you are finished let the piece dry completely.

STEP 8: Place the painted cover unit on your ironing surface with the colored side face down on a sheet of parchment paper. Place the remaining piece of Mistyfuse onto the Stiffy surface. Next place the lining fabric over the Mistyfuse with the right side face up. Cover with another sheet of parchment paper. Press well to fuse the lining in place. Then flip the unit over and iron the other side to heat set the color.

STEP 9: Cut the three cover pieces apart. Cut the front and back pieces to 9" x 6". Cut the spine to 1½" x 9". Because the quilted areas were oversized to begin with, you can nudge your ruler around to find the best areas for cutting into your cover pieces.

STEP 10: Zigzag stitch around the four edges of each cover piece. It is important to set your zigzag stitch so it is not a very dense stitch, like a satin stitch. You will be stitching along all the edges a second time, so you don't want the stitching too heavy.

STEP 11: Position the covers on your work table so they are in the correct configuration for joining. The outside fabric should be face up. See diagram.

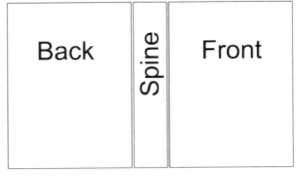

| Back | Spine | Front |

Starting with the spine and front cover, push the two pieces together so they touch but don't overlap. Set your machine to a wide zigzag stitch and stitch the pieces together. Flip the unit over and stitch the same seam a second time. Add the back cover to the other edge of the spine piece in the same way.

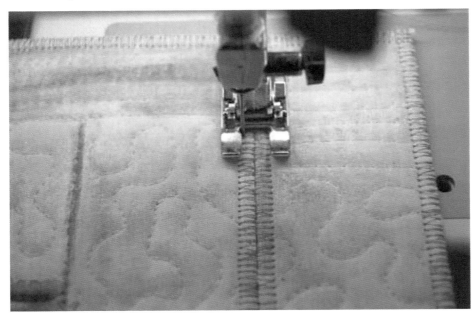

Once all three pieces are stitched together, zigzag stitch around the outside edge of the entire unit one more time. Adjust your zigzag stitch length accordingly for the desired amount of stitch coverage.

STEP 12: Prepare five signatures for the inside pages of your journal using paper measuring 8½" x 11" and folded in half to make pages 8½" x 5½".

Using a four-hole punching guide as described in *Making and Sewing Signatures* beginning on page 21, punch the holes in your signatures.

Open up the journal cover and with the lining side up, center your hole-punching guide (made with 5 columns of holes for this project) over the spine section and mark and punch your holes.

Thread a tapestry needle with an 18" length of embroidery floss, linen twine or other sturdy thread and sew in the signatures following the four-hole stitching pattern on page 26.

Tip: The spine on this book can be adjusted in width to make a smaller book or a larger book. Allow ⅜" to ¼" width for each signature you add or remove.

Tip: An assortment of paint-brushes is helpful for painting and spreading the water-soluble crayons in areas on the surface. Some areas may be small and narrow, while others may be large. Paintbrushes in assorted sizes and shapes will help achieve painting success.

Paintbrushes with a lot of flexibility don't work as well as those that are a little less flexible for brushing the color on the fabric. A favorite paintbrush for this technique is a short-bristled brush known as a chisel blender.

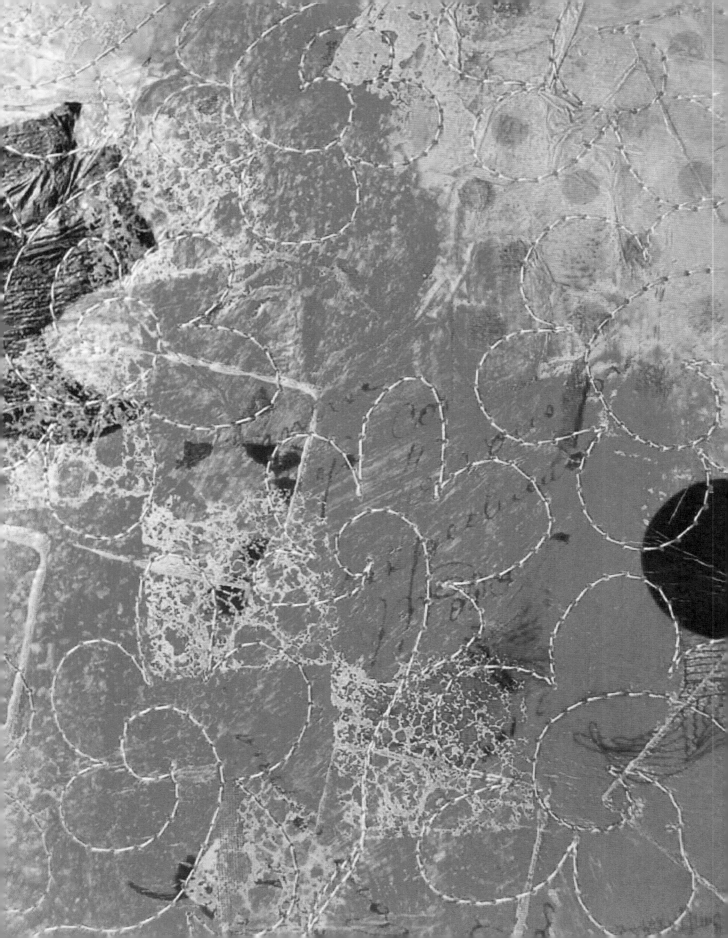

CHAPTER 5

Collaged Surfaces

Paper Fabric Journal

Mixing paper and fabric together is becoming very popular and makes for an exciting surface that you can use for many types of projects. The unique touches you can add to your paper fabric surface is unlimited and only limited by your own imagination.

SUPPLIES NEEDED

Muslin or any cotton fabric
Paper (see types, page 47)
White craft glue
Mixing cup
Plastic spoon
Paintbrushes - 1" and 2" wide
Acrylic paint
Stamps and stencils
Timtex
Parchment paper
Mistyfuse
Fabric to line the inside of your journal
Paper for the inside pages of the journal

STEP 1: Create the paper fabric surface. Cut a piece of muslin 18" x 22". You will have extra paper fabric left over for another project after making your book.

Place the muslin on a protected work surface and smooth it out flat. A plastic or vinyl covered surface works best, because when the paper fabric is dry it peels away easily.

Mix a 50/50 solution of white craft glue and water with the plastic spoon in a mixing cup. With a 2" paintbrush, brush the glue solution onto the muslin to completely cover and saturate it.

Start placing torn paper pieces onto the wet muslin. You can cover the muslin completely or leave some fabric peeking through.

Brush the glue solution on the papers as you put them on the muslin or place a few randomly across the surface and brush glue solution over a few at a time. This helps the other papers adhere if there is any overlap. When you are happy with the amount of paper coverage on your muslin, gently brush glue solution over the entire paper and fabric surface. Don't worry if you get a small tear. You can leave it or cover it with another piece of paper. Let the paper fabric dry thoroughly, usually overnight.

Tip: You can save leftover glue solution by storing it in an airtight container. You will need to mix it well when you want to use it again.

STEP 2: Once the surface is dry, you can add color and other design details. Using acrylic paint and the 1" paintbrush, add color over the surface of the paper. If using more than one color, gently blend the colors where they meet. Use transparent paints so that any design that is printed on the tissue paper shows through. Let dry.

STEP 3: Using complimentary, contrasting, or metallic acrylic paint; add stamped or stenciled designs to the paper surface. Let dry.

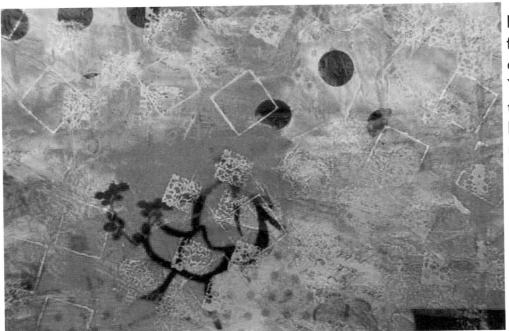

Remove the paper fabric from the plastic covered workspace. You will notice that the paper fabric will have a tendency to curl up. You can easily iron it flat. Sandwich the paper fabric between parchment paper to protect your iron and ironing surface.

STEP 4: Cut the Timtex and one piece of Mistyfuse to 10" x 15½". Place the Misty-fuse on one side of the Timtex and cover with parchment paper. Press with a hot iron to fuse. Let cool and remove the parchment paper.

Tip: You may need to press and hold a bit longer when fusing the paper fabric to the Timtex. The thickness of the paper fabric may need more heating time.

Cut your paper fabric slightly larger than the Timtex. Place the paper fabric, wrong side down on the Timtex with the pre-applied Mistyfuse. Cover with the parchment paper and press with your iron to bond the paper fabric to the Timtex.

Trim the excess paper fabric away from the Timtex.

Tip: Remember to always use parchment paper when fusing with Mistyfuse. If you should happen to get a stray piece of Mistyfuse on the sole plate of your iron, you can clean it off by ironing an unused dryer sheet.

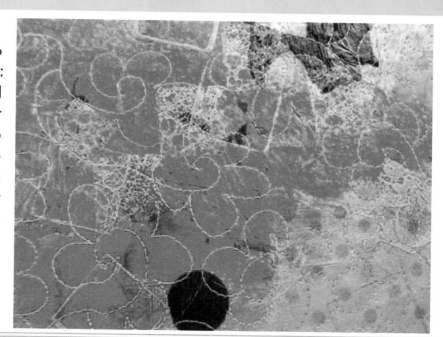

STEP 5: Add stitching to the paper fabric surface. Note: This step is optional. The quilted stitching lines add another layer of interest as well as texture to the finished cover. This stitching can be done in a free-motion technique or you can use your machine's straight, zigzag, or decorative stitches.

PAPER TYPES

Tissue paper is a favorite paper to use. Save tissue you receive in gifts or packages. Because it is inexpensive you can even shop in the gift wrap section of your store to look for interesting tissue paper that will look great in your projects. Keep in mind though, that you can use any paper you like, such as newspaper, old book pages, telephone book pages, napkins, decorative papers, ephemera, pages from your notebooks, and more.

STEP 6: Cut the Timtex cover to 9" x 14¼". Cut a piece of Mistyfuse to this same measurement and fuse it to the other side of the Timtex.

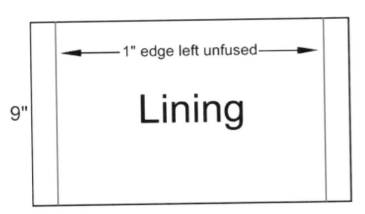

Cut the lining fabric slightly larger than the Timtex piece. Place the lining fabric wrong side down against the Timtex, cover with parchment paper and iron to fuse the fabric to the Timtex. Don't iron the two 9" edges of the lining fabric. Iron so that about 1" on each end is left unfused. See diagram. Trim away the excess lining fabric.

STEP 7: Add the closure loops. The closure for this journal is made with two loops of fabric. You could also use elastic if you desire.

To prepare the loops from fabric, cut a piece of fabric 2½" x 6". Fold the strip in half lengthwise and stitch with a ¼" seam allowance down the 6" raw edges to form a tube. Turn the tube right side out and press so the seam runs down the middle of the strip. Topstitch the two long edges of the strip, stitching ⅛" in from the edge. Cut two pieces from this strip that measure 2" long. Fold these in half with the seam to the inside, and press.

Slip the folded loop under the unfused lining. You will need to judge how far under the lining to position the loop so that your loop ends up large enough for a pen/pencil to fit through.

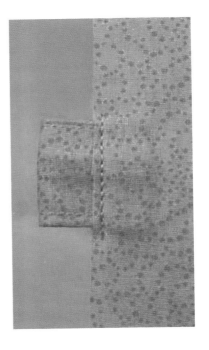

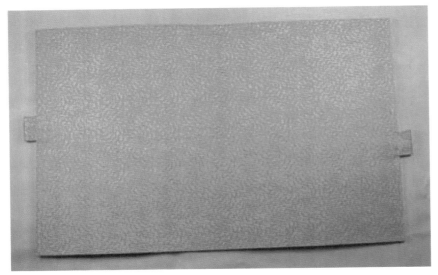

When the loop is in the position you want, press with your iron to fuse the rest of the lining fabric down around and over the loop. Place a loop of fabric on each end of the cover, offsetting them. After you have fused the lining down, straight stitch over the loop to secure it. Place this stitching about ⅛" from the edge of the journal cover.

STEP 8: Finish all four edges of the journal with a zigzag stitch. Stitch right over the loops as if they aren't there.

STEP 9: Prepare three signatures for the inside pages of your journal using paper measuring 8½" x 11" and folded in half to make pages 8½" x 5½".

Using a three- or four-hole punching guide as described in *Making and Sewing Signatures* beginning on page 21, punch the holes in your signatures.

The signatures will be centered on the inside of the book. Using your hole-punching guide, mark the hole placement on the lining.

Thread a tapestry needle with an 18" length of embroidery floss, linen twine or other sturdy thread and sew in the signatures following the appropriate stitching pattern on pages 26 and 27.

Fabric Collage Journal

Fused, raw-edge applique is a perfect technique for using up small bits of fabrics to create a fabulous design for your journal cover. Add some quilting for texture and your results are simply stunning.

SUPPLIES NEEDED

Timtex or Peltex
Mistyfuse
Parchment paper
Assortment of fabrics for cover design
Fabric for lining the inside of the journal
Drawing paper
Permanent marker
Freezer paper
1" piece of Velcro
Button
Paper for the inside pages of the journal

STEP 1: Cut the Timtex, lining fabric and two pieces of Mistyfuse to measure 18" x 9". Set aside the lining fabric and one sheet of Mistyfuse for later.

STEP 2: Fuse a piece of Mistyfuse to one side of the Timtex by placing the Timtex and Mistyfuse between two sheets of parchment paper to create a sandwich. Press with a hot iron to bond the Mistyfuse to the Timtex. Let cool and remove the parchment paper.

STEP 3: Draw the design for your journal on a sheet of paper. Start by drawing a rectangle 18" x 9". This is the area that you'll draw your design in.

Next measure in from the left and mark a 3" dashed line. This area is the flap that folds over to the front of the journal. You can give this area any shape you wish.

Measure in 2" from the right side and mark a dashed line. This area is usually covered by the flap when the journal is closed, so you may

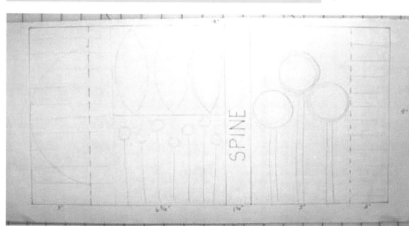

want to keep major design elements outside this area. From the right side measure 7" in and mark a line. This is one edge of your spine. Measure over another 1¼" to 1½" for the other spine edge.

The areas you have marked are the major division or fold lines. It is helpful to mark these with a marker so they are permanent and you don't accidently erase them while you're drawing.

STEP 4: Using a pencil, sketch in your design and the shape you would like your flap to be. This drawing is now your map or pattern.

STEP 5: Mark the major division lines on your Timtex. With the Mistyfuse side face up, mark with a pencil the lines that you have marked in marker on your map. Also mark any

other dividing lines you've created, such as the horizontal line in the photo. Note that the lines in the photo are made with marker for you to see them better. A light pencil mark is all that's needed. If you use a light-colored fabric on top of your lines, a line made with marker may show.

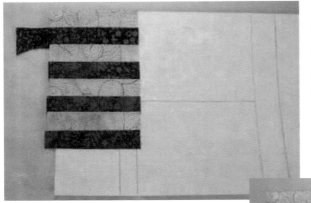

STEP 6: Following your map, start placing fabrics on your Timtex piece starting with your background pieces first. Measure the dimensions of the section you are covering with fabric and add approximately ¼" for overlap. Work from the right and left edges toward the spine and cover the spine last. Be sure your fabric pieces overlap so that no Timtex is peeking through.

STEP 7: When all your background fabrics are in place, cover the piece carefully with a sheet of parchment paper and press with your iron to fuse them to the Timtex. Let cool and remove the parchment.

Trim away any fabrics that extend beyond the edge of the Timtex.

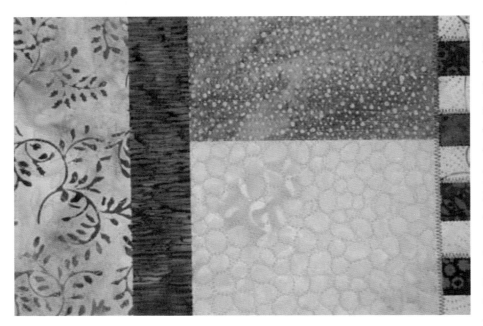

STEP 8: Add quilting or background stitching. This can be accomplished in many ways. Free-motion quilting is a great method to cover the background fabrics. You can also use your machine's straight, zigzag, or pre-programmed decorative stitches.

You may want to zigzag stitch over the raw edges on your piece to secure them in place. The sample shown has been stitched with both free-motion quilting and machine-guided stitches. Another option is hand stitching.

STEP 9: Add your focal design elements. Trace your designs onto the non-shiny side of freezer paper with a pencil or marker. If you have trouble seeing your map's penciled drawings under the freezer paper, darken them with a marker.

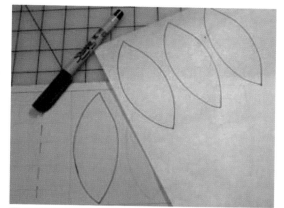

Cut the patterns from the freezer paper, but don't cut on the lines. Allow some margin around each drawn element.

Place the freezer paper pattern on your chosen fabric so that the shiny side of the freezer paper is against the right side of the fabric. With your iron, press the paper onto the fabric. The paper will stick to the fabric, but it will easily peel away when you want to remove it and will leave no residue.

Cut out the section of fabric with the freezer paper on it and place it, freezer paper side down, on top of a sheet of parchment paper on your ironing surface. Cut a piece of Mistyfuse approximately the same size as the piece of fabric that your templates are adhered to. Place the Mistyfuse on the fabric, lay another sheet of parchment paper on top and press with your iron to fuse.

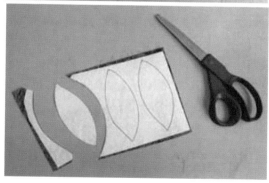

Now you can cut your fabric shapes. Cut along the lines you have drawn. Peel the freezer paper away and place the applique piece on your Timtex in the location you have mapped out.

You can use the freezer paper template method with all of your design elements or you can simply apply some Mistyfuse to the wrong side of your chosen fabric and free hand cut your shapes. Once your design elements are all in place, carefully cover them with a sheet of parchment paper and press with your iron to bond them in place.

Once all the pieces are fused in place, return to the sewing machine to add stitching around the edges of your design elements and any other decorative stitching you would like. You can also hand stitch if you prefer.

STEP 10: Place the journal shell on your ironing surface, on top of a piece of parchment paper. Place it so the outside fabric is face down. Take the piece of Mistyfuse you set aside earlier and position it on the Timtex. Cover with the lining fabric, placed right side up and then cover the entire Timtex unit with parchment paper. Press with your iron to bond the lining fabric to the Timtex. Let cool and remove the parchment paper. Trim away any excess lining fabric that extends beyond the Timtex edges.

STEP 11: Cut the flap shape. You can transfer your flap shape markings to your journal shell by creating a template or by simply drawing on the journal shell with a pencil or chalk marker. Be sure you are cutting the flap shape on the correct end of the journal shell.

STEP 12: Attach the Velcro. Stitch one piece of your Velcro to the outside journal shell. This piece will be on the front cover area of the journal shell. Place it accordingly to your flap design. On the sample shown, the Velcro was stitched in the center of the 9" edge and placed ½" from the edge. Take your second piece of Velcro and stitch it to the lining side of your flap. Again, place it according to where your outside piece of Velcro is positioned.

STEP 13: Prepare an optional pocket by cutting a piece of fabric 6½" square. Fold the fabric, wrong sides together, on the diagonal and press well.

Position the pocket on the lining as shown. It should be on the inside left side of the front cover. Align the raw edges of the pocket with the raw edges of the Timtex and pin it in place.

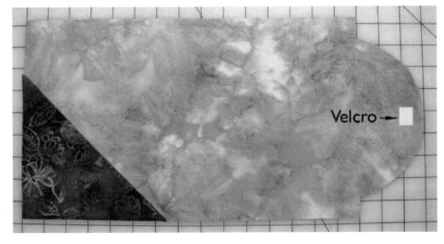

STEP 14: Zigzag stitch around the entire journal shell, making sure to catch the raw edges of the pocket.

STEP 15: Add a decorative element, such as a button, to the outside flap to hide the area where the Velcro was stitched.

STEP 16: Prepare four signatures for the inside pages of your journal using paper measuring 8½" x 11" and folded in half to make pages 8½" x 5½".

Using a four-hole punching guide as described in *Making and Sewing Signatures* beginning on page 21, punch the holes in your signatures.

Fold your journal shell so that it is correctly aligned for your flap to close. Open up the journal cover and with the lining side up, center your hole punching guide (made with 4 columns of holes for this project) over the spine section and mark and punch your holes.

Thread a tapestry needle with an 18" length of embroidery floss, linen twine or other sturdy thread and sew in the signatures following the four-hole stitching pattern on page 26.

Tip: Fold the journal shell and flap to their closed position and press with your iron. This will set the folds and ensures the journal will close correctly each time.

CHAPTER 6

Textured Surfaces

Linen & Pearls Journal

Linen is wonderful fabric to work with and is perfect for creating the frayed edges that give this journal a soft, tactile surface that's a joy to hold in your hand. You'll find it in a wide range of colors but the neutral and natural colors work particularly well for this journal. The addition of the smooth pearl beads adds a nice contrast to the soft frayed edges of the linen. This journal would make a lovely gift for a bride-to-be to record all her wedding memories in.

SUPPLIES NEEDED

Linen fabric
Timtex
Fabric to line the inside of your journal
Mistyfuse
Parchment paper
Pearl beads
Paper for the inside pages of the journal

STEP 1: Cut your linen fabric into strips ranging from ½" to 1" wide by 11" long. Reserve a piece of linen 10" x 20" to use as a base to sew your strips to.

STEP 2: Sew the linen strips to your base fabric using thread in a coordinating color. Sew down the middle of each strip placing the strips next to each other and remember to backstitch at the top and bottom of each strip so that they don't come off in the next step.

STEP 3: When the entire surface of the base fabric is covered with strips toss the piece into the washer with a couple of towels, and then into the dryer. When you take it out of the dryer it will be a frayed mess of threads—that's good!

STEP 4: Trim off some of the excess threads and then fuse your fabric to a piece of Timtex that is cut 8" x 16". Trim off any excess fabric extending beyond the edges of the Timtex.

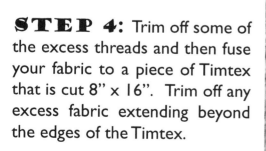

STEP 5: Sew the pearl beads to the journal keeping them ½" from the edges.

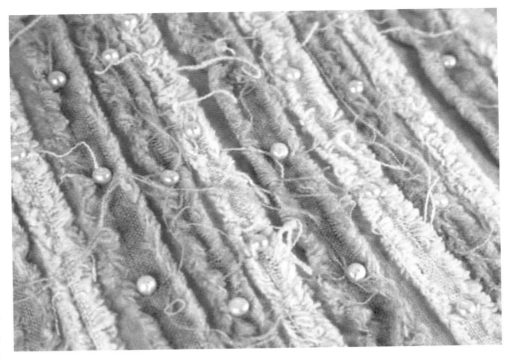

STEP 6: Fuse a lining fabric to the other side of the journal and then finish the edges of the journal with a zigzag stitch.

STEP 7: Prepare three signatures for the inside of your journal using paper measuring 7½" x 14" and folded in half to make pages 7½" x 7". Using a four-hole punching guide as described in *Making and Sewing Signatures* beginning on page 21, punch the holes in your signatures. For paper signatures this size, the recommended hole placement is: 1" from the top, 2¾" from the top, 4¾" from the top and 6½" from the top.

Open up the journal cover and with the lining side up, place your hole-punching guide about 7¾" in from the left edge and punch the holes in the journal cover.

Thread a tapestry needle with an 18" length of embroidery floss, linen twine or other sturdy thread and sew in the signatures following the four-hole stitching pattern on page 26.

TRY THIS: Instead of using linen for this journal consider using some denim material. Perhaps you've got some old jeans laying around in the closet that don't fit anymore or have too many holes in them to wear. Cut them apart and then cut them into strips and stitch them to your base fabric. You may have to send it through the wash cycle more than once to encourage the strips to fray. The resulting journal would make a great gift for a teen headed off to college to use as a scrapbook.

Tip: If you would like to add some pearl beads along the stitching of the spine but your needle is too large to fit through the bead holes, sew the signatures in first and then sew them in again using a beading needle and thread that will fit through the beads you want to use.

Tip: Consider adding some color to your pages by brushing the edges with some walnut ink. This lends a nice accent to the overall vintage feel of the journal.

Silk Journal with a Twist

This journal is a great way to use up some leftover fabric scraps from the silk Shibori journal shown on page 30, but any fabric you have on hand will work well for this. Cotton, organza and even strips of linen will work very nicely and create a lovely textural surface with this technique.

SUPPLIES NEEDED

For making the machine cord:
  Fabric
  Sewing machine
  Thread

For making the journal:
  Timtex
  Fabric to line the inside of your journal
  Mistyfuse
  Parchment paper
  Button cover kit
  Paper for the inside pages of the journal
  4" elastic cording
  Textile paints, optional

It's a good idea to make a test cord first before you tear all of your fabric into strips. I found that a 1" strip worked perfectly for silk fabric but you may want to use a larger strip if you're working with cotton or linen.

STEP 1: Tear your fabric into the desired strip sizes and then set your machine up with a wide zigzag stitch.

STEP 2: Working with one strip of fabric at a time, loosely twist it and place one end under the needle on the sewing machine a few inches in from the end of the fabric. You'll need to leave that extra few inches free so that you have something to hold onto when you start stitching.

I like to use a shiny rayon thread when I make machine cord, but cotton will work fine and metallics will add a bit of bling to your finished cord.

Tip: You'll need to make a generous amount of machine cord depending on the journal size you want to make and be sure to make more than you think you need so you don't come up short!

Make sure you choose a coordinating thread for the bobbin since it will show on the finished cord.

Start stitching! As you stitch you will need to continue to twist the fabric and pull it through the machine since the feed dogs may not be much help.

How fast or slow you pull the fabric through will determine what kind of thread coverage you get. It's not necessary to completely cover the cord and it's not important to make your stitches even and neat!

When you have a nice pile of machine cording done you can start creating the surface for your journal. Cut

a piece of Timtex to measure 6" x 12". You can paint the Timtex with textile paints if you like. I've painted mine with some black textile paint so that if I'm not exact when I stitch down my machine cord the white surface of the Timtex won't show through.

STEP 3: Place a length of machine cord on the Timtex leaving about 2" of the cord hanging off the short edge to use as fringe in the finished journal. Use a zigzag stitch to sew the cording in place.

Continue sewing strips of cording to the Timtex until you've completely covered the surface. If your strips are not long enough to go all the way across the surface just overlap the ends a bit and keep stitching.

If you have some cord left over, you can use it to add some additional visual interest to the surface of the journal by stitching a swirl pattern over the top.

STEP 4: Once your cording is all stitched to the surface use Mistyfuse to fuse a piece of fabric to the other side of the Timtex. This is the lining of your journal.

STEP 5: Prepare three signatures for the inside of your journal using paper measuring 5½" x 10½" and folded in half to make signatures measuring 5½" x 5¼".

Using a four-hole punching guide as described in *Making and Sewing Signatures* beginning on page 21, punch the holes in your signatures. For paper signatures this size, the recommended hole placement is: ½" from the top, then 2" from the top, 3½" from the top and 5" from the top.

Open up the journal cover and with the lining side up, place your hole-punching guide about 5¾" in from the left edge and punch the holes in the journal cover.

Thread a tapestry needle with an 18" length of embroidery floss, linen twine or other sturdy thread and sew in the signatures following the four-hole stitching pattern on page 26.

STEP 6: To create the fringe along the edges of the journal use a seam ripper to remove any excess stitching along the cording that extends beyond the edge of journal.

STEP 7: Add a button to the outside of your journal by using a button cover kit to create a coordinating button for the outside. Punch a small hole ¾" in from the edge of the back cover of the journal. Center the hole between the top and bottom edge. Fold the elastic in half and tie the ends together. Push the loop through the hole from the inside to the outside and then loop the elastic around the button on the front of the journal.

CHAPTER 7

Mixed-Media Surfaces

Tissue Paper Surface Journal

This technique creates a wonderfully textured surface. Using Tim-tex as the substrate for the surface gives the finished result a good amount of flexibility making it perfect for a wrap-around journal style.

SUPPLIES NEEDED

Timtex
White tissue paper
Golden white gesso
Chip brush
Foam brush
Rubber gloves
Golden soft gel gloss
Paint
Mistyfuse
Parchment paper
Fabric to line the inside of your journal
Velcro
Paper for the inside pages of the journal

STEP 1: Before you begin you need to prepare the gesso. Straight out of the bottle the Golden gesso is a little too thick to use for this technique and it needs to be thinned with some water first. Use a 2 to 1 mix of gesso to water and stir it well to combine. If you use a different brand then you may want to add more or less water depending on how thick it is out of the jar. It should be about the consistency of skim milk. If it's thinned too much it won't have enough bonding strength and if it's not thinned enough then the resulting surface will be too stiff.

STEP 2: Cut a piece of Timtex 10" x 20". This is a little larger than you need and you'll be trimming it to size later.

STEP 3: Brush one side of the Timtex with the gesso/water mixture. The surface should be covered with the mixture but not sopping wet.

Crumple a piece of tissue paper up in your hands and then open it up and place it on the surface of the Timtex. You don't have to completely smooth it out onto the surface and it doesn't have to completely cover it either.

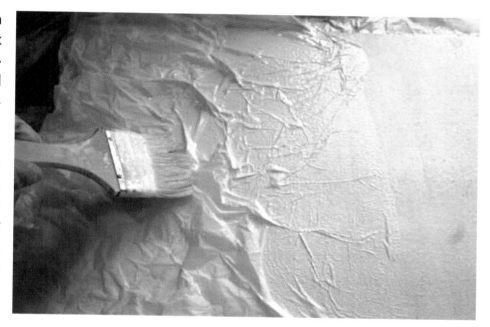

Brush a layer of the gesso/water mixture all over the tissue to adhere it to the surface. The tissue may tear, but that's okay and don't worry about the wrinkles and bumps. You want those, they add the nice texture to the finished surface.

Tip: This is a messy technique. You may want to wear a pair of gloves to avoid getting gesso all over your hands.

If your piece of tissue wasn't large enough to cover the entire piece of Timtex just add some pieces to the bare spots and brush over them with the gesso/water mixture.

Tip: It's a good idea to let your tissue fall over the edges of the Timtex You'll be trimming it later so don't worry about the messy edges. By letting the tissue fall over the edge you'll insure that the entire piece is covered and won't lift off when you cut it to size later.

When you have covered the surface with tissue add another layer of crumpled tissue on top and press it into the surface. Brush on some more gesso/water mixture and make sure that the entire piece of tissue has been painted with the mixture.

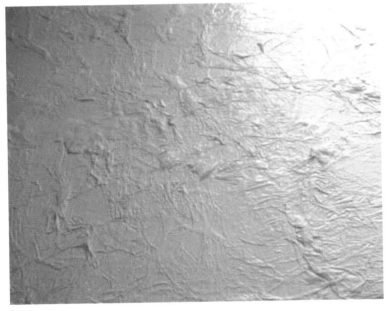

Repeat this gesso/water and tissue layering until you are happy with the way the surface looks. Too many layers makes the result too stiff, so aim for three to four total layers. If you have any gaps or holes just tear off a piece of tissue and paint it on. When you think you are done adding tissue, go over the surface with your hands and press out any large air bubbles. Don't smooth the surface out too much, you want the texture. You just don't want any large air bubbles on the surface.

Set the piece aside to dry. It's important for it to be completely dry before you paint it so don't rush this process and let it dry undisturbed for at least 12 hours or overnight.

STEP 4: Once it's dry you can paint it. Just about any type of paint will work for this. Acrylics, textile, watercolor or even spray inks will work just fine.

This piece is painted with a copper acrylic paint and then some light dabs of turquoise were added on the surface.

After you've added color to the surface set it aside again to dry completely. When it's dry trim it to measure 9" x 18" and it's ready to be turned into a journal.

STEP 5: Use Mistyfuse to fuse your lining fabric to the other side of the surface. If you want your journal to have a decorative edge on the flap you'll want to cut that now. With the journal shell lining side up cut the right edge of the journal shell in a shape you like.

Tip: To finish the edges of the surface and cover the white edge of the Timtex, dab a little paint around the edges. You can use a sponge brush to apply a light layer of paint all around the edges. You can alternatively use a marker or a rubber stamp pad for this.

STEP 6: Seal the textured tissue surface with two light coats of Golden soft gel gloss, letting it dry between coats. Use a foam brush instead of a chip brush for this and you'll get better coverage and less puddles of the medium on the surface.

STEP 7: Add a Velcro closure to the journal shell. Cut a piece of Velcro 1¼" long and with the lining side up, place one side of the Velcro on the right side centered between the top and bottom and ½" from the edge.

Sew the other piece of Velcro to the other side of the journal shell on the outside. Center it halfway between the top and bottom edges and place it about ¾" in from the edge.

STEP 8: Prepare three signatures for the inside of your journal using paper measuring 8½" x 11" and folded in half to make pages 5½" x 8½".

Using a four-hole punching guide as described in *Making and Sewing Signatures* beginning on page 21, punch the holes in your signatures.

Open up the journal cover and with the lining side up, place your hole-punching guide about 6½" in from the left edge and punch the holes in the journal cover.

Thread a tapestry needle with an 18" length of embroidery floss, linen twine or other sturdy thread and sew in the signatures following the four-hole stitching pattern on page 26.

STEP 9: Add a decorative button or other embellishment to the front flap to cover the stitching lines where you sewed on the Velcro.

Tip: Experiment with different colors and paints with this technique. Metallic paints create an exciting, luminous surface whereas watercolor sprays result in a softer, pastel look. This green journal was painted with Lumiere paint in metallic olive green.

Tip: If you would rather not use Velcro as a closure for your journal, tie a button onto the front flap and use a length of suede, leather or even paper cording as a wrap tie close instead.

Recycled Envelope Journal

With so much emphasis on going green these days, this journal surface fits right in. It's fun to save the envelopes that come in the mail and it's a special treat when you get one that has a new printed pattern.

SUPPLIES NEEDED

Timtex
Recycled envelopes with printed patterns
Fabric to line the inside of your journal
Mistyfuse
Parchment paper
Portfolio Series water-soluble oil pastels
Paintbrush
Matte acrylic medium
Saved postage stamps, stickers or other
    paper ephemera
2 - One-inch D-rings
12" of 5/8" or 3/4" grosgrain ribbon
Paper for the inside pages of the journal

STEP 1: Cut one piece of Timtex, two pieces of Mistyfuse, and one piece of lining fabric to 9½" x 14". Set aside the lining fabric and one piece of Mistyfuse for later.

STEP 2: Create a sandwich on your ironing surface. The layers of the sandwich are from bottom to top: sheet of parchment paper, Timtex, Mistyfuse, parchment paper. Press with your iron to bond the Mistyfuse to the Timtex. Let cool and remove the top sheet of parchment paper.

STEP 3: Open up the envelopes at the glued seams. Tear the envelope paper into 1" to 2" pieces. If you don't have patterned envelope paper, you can substitute decorative paper, such as scrapbook paper. You will want to use patterned paper that has a white or light-colored background.

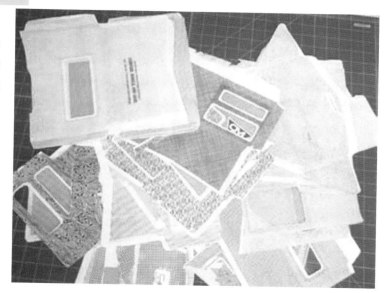

Tip: Have friends and relatives save patterned envelopes for you. You will have a greater chance at collecting different patterns.

STEP 4: Starting at one end of the Timtex, with the Mistyfuse side face up, start placing the torn pieces of envelope paper. Overlap the envelope paper slightly so that no Timtex peeks through.

As you work your way across the Timtex surface, you can periodically press with your iron to secure the paper. Very carefully cover the surface with parchment paper and press to fuse the papers down. Let cool, remove the parchment paper, and continue placing the torn papers to

completely cover the surface. Be sure to give a good press with your iron when the entire Timtex surface is covered.

STEP 5: Choose three colors of water-soluble oil pastels and add random blocks of each color to the envelope surface. Completely cover the surface with color.

With a cup of water and the paintbrush, dip the brush into the water and start brushing water over the surface. The oil pastel will "melt" and spread as you brush. After you have brushed water over the entire surface and blended the colors a bit, let it dry. Once it's dry you can go over any areas again where you would like more or deeper color.

Tip: You can substitute water-soluble crayons or transparent acrylic paints for the water-soluble oil pastels.

STEP 6: You can add further surface design with stamped and stenciled designs and acrylic paint or stamp pad ink. Another option for more surface interest is to adhere saved postage stamps randomly across the surface. Brush matte acrylic medium on the backside of the postage stamp and place on the envelope surface. Then brush more acrylic medium over the top of the stamp. If you don't have any interesting postage stamps saved, you could use other paper ephemera or even stickers.

STEP 7: Add stitched texture to the envelope surface. You can add texture to the surface with either a free-motion stitching technique or with the straight, zigzag or decorative stitches on your sewing machine.

STEP 8: Place the stitched envelope surface on your ironing surface with the colored side face down on a sheet of parchment paper. Place the remaining piece of Mistyfuse onto the Timtex. Place the lining fabric over the Mistyfuse with the right side face up and cover with another sheet of parchment paper. Press well to fuse the lining in place. Leave approximately

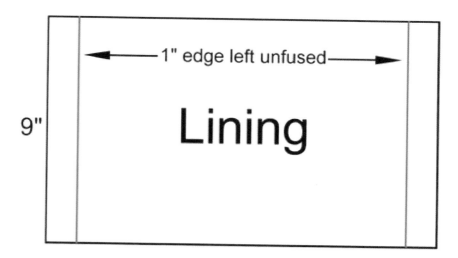

one inch of lining fabric unfused on the two short ends (see diagram). This is where you will insert the grosgrain ribbon ends.

STEP 9: Trim the journal cover to 9" x 13".

STEP 10: Cut 2" from the 12" length of grosgrain ribbon. Place the two D-rings onto this 2" piece. Fold the ribbon in half and insert the two cut ends under the lining fabric. You can place the D-rings on either the front or back cover. For the example shown, the D-rings are attached to the front cover.

Tip: You can substitute a sewn fabric strip for grosgrain ribbon.

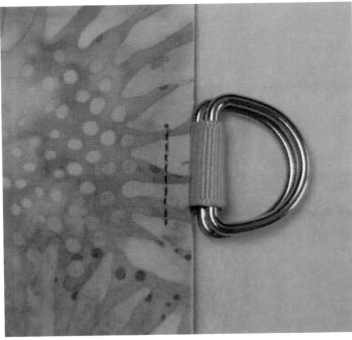

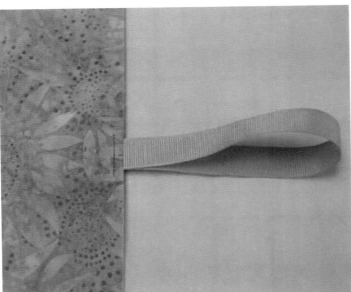

When inserting the ribbon under the lining fabric, center it along the edge of the cover. Don't push too much of the ribbon under the lining fabric because you want the D-rings to be able to move freely.

Stitch a straight stitch to secure the ribbon in place. Position the stitching approximately ⅛" from the edge of the Tim-tex cover.

Fold the remaining 10" of grosgrain ribbon in half to form a loop. Insert the two cut ends of the loop under the lining on the opposite end of the journal cover centering it along the edge. Push the ends under the lining about ½" or so and straight stitch to secure.

Press with your iron to completely fuse down the lining that was left un-fused.

STEP 11: Finish all four edges of the journal with a zigzag stitch. Stitch right over the ribbons as if they aren't there.

STEP 12: Prepare three signatures for the inside of your journal using paper measuring 8½" x 11" and folded in half to make pages 5½" x 8½".

Using a four-hole punching guide as described in *Making and Sewing Signatures* beginning on page 21, punch the holes in your signatures.

The signatures will be centered on the inside of the book. Using your hole-punching guide, mark the hole placement on the lining. Stitch the signatures to the journal cover following the stitching guidelines on page 26.

CHAPTER 8

Hard Cover Books

Mini Basic Hard Cover Book

This small, hard cover book is the perfect size for tucking into a travel bag, book bag or purse.

SUPPLIES NEEDED

Book board:
  Two pieces 6" x 4¾" (front and back)
  One piece 6" x 1½" (spine)

Book cloth 8" x 3"

NOTE: You can substitute decorative paper or a piece of starched cotton or other fabric for book cloth.

If your cotton or fabric is thin consider using a fusible interfacing on the wrong side to prevent the glue from seeping through.

Decorative paper for the outside:
  Two pieces 8" x 6½"

Decorative paper (or book cloth) for lining the inside of your book
Glue stick or white PVA glue
Paper for the inside pages of the journal
Tapestry or heavy duty sewing needle
Ribbon

STEP 1: Place your 8" x 3" book cloth piece on your work surface right side down. Apply glue to one side of the spine piece, cut from the book board, and center it on the book cloth, glue side down.

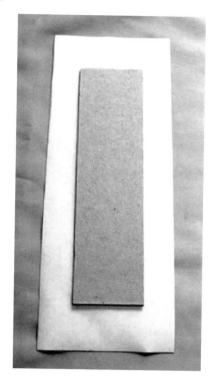

STEP 2: Apply glue along the edge of the book cloth keeping it about 1" from the

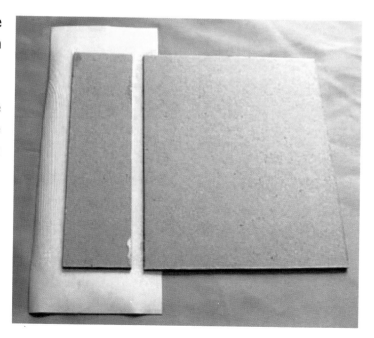

top and bottom edge and place one of the cover pieces, cut from the book board, on the book cloth.

Place the book board along the glued edge keeping it ¼" from the edge of the spine piece and keeping the top and bottom edges aligned.

Glue the other piece of book board to the other side of the book cloth.

STEP 3: Put some glue along the excess book cloth extending beyond the top and bottom edges of the book and fold these edges over to the inside. Press them down very well to make sure they are attached securely to the book board.

STEP 4: Turn your book over so that the right side is facing you and coat one side with glue, but do not put any glue on the book cloth.

Take one piece of your decorative paper and determine which edge will overlap the book cloth edge.

Turn the paper over and run a line of glue about ½" wide along the edge on the wrong side of the paper.

Tip: It's important to note that if you're using a paper with a directional pattern that you determine which edge will be along the spine before you apply any glue to the paper.

Place the paper on the book cover where you have applied the glue. Place the paper on the cover so that the left edge of your paper overlaps over the edge of the book cloth by about ¼" and the paper extends beyond the top and bottom edges of the book cover by about 1". There will be more than 1" of paper extending beyond the right edge, but that's okay because you'll trim the excess off later.

Press the paper down very well to be sure that there are no wrinkles or air bubbles and that the paper is in good contact with the cover.

Repeat these steps to apply the decorative paper to the other side of the book cover.

STEP 5: When you have glued both sides of the cover papers on, flip the book over so that the inside is facing up and trim the paper edges to 1". Then turn in the corners and edges and glue them in place.

STEP 6: Cut two pieces of ribbon 8" long and glue them to the inside of the book, approximately 2" in from the edge.

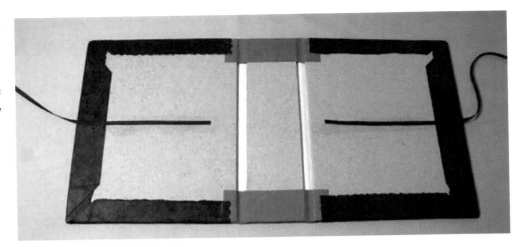

STEP 7: Cut a piece of paper measuring 5½" x 11¼" to line the inside of your book and glue it in place.

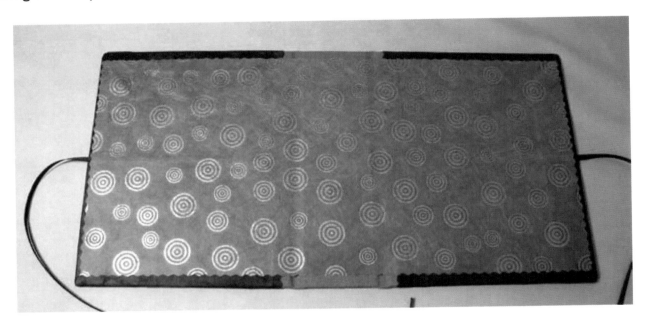

Set the book aside while you prepare your signatures for the inside.

STEP 8: Prepare three signatures for the inside of your journal using paper measuring 8½" x 5½" and folded in half to make a page 4¼" x 5½".

Using a four-hole punching guide as described in *Making and Sewing Signatures* beginning on page 21, punch the holes in your signatures. This book is a bit smaller than the example in that chapter, so place your holes at ¾" from the top and bottom of the page and then 2" from the top and bottom of the page.

Open up the book cover and with the lining side up, center your hole-punching guide along the center of the spine and punch the holes in the book cover.

Thread a tapestry needle with an 18" length of embroidery floss, linen twine or other sturdy thread and sew in the signatures following the four-hole stitching pattern on page 26 .

Enjoy writing in your new book!

Fabric Strip Book

Creating a hard cover book with fabric strips gives a soft, feminine feeling to your book.

SUPPLIES NEEDED

Book board:
   Two pieces 6" x 9" (front and back)
   One piece 9" x 1½" (spine)
Book cloth 11" x 3"
Paper to line the inside of your book
Fabric strips
Tear-away stabilizer 11½" x 14½"
Glue stick or white PVA glue
Paper for the inside pages of the book
Elastic cord closure - Optional

STEP 1: Create your fabric strip cover by tearing strips of fabric that are at least 12" long and approximately 1" to 1½" wide. You will need enough strips to completely cover the piece of tear-away stabilizer.

Tear a few strips of a coordinating or contrasting fabric. Make these strips narrower. Tear them approximately ½" to ¾" wide and at least 12" long.

STEP 2: Sew your 1" to 1½" wide fabric strips to the tear-away stabilizer. Starting at one end of the stabilizer, position the strip so it extends slightly off the edge of the stabilizer and sew with a wide zigzag stitch down the center of the strip. Add the next strip and overlap the strips by approximately ⅛" to ¼". Continue adding strips in this manner until the stabilizer is completely covered with strips.

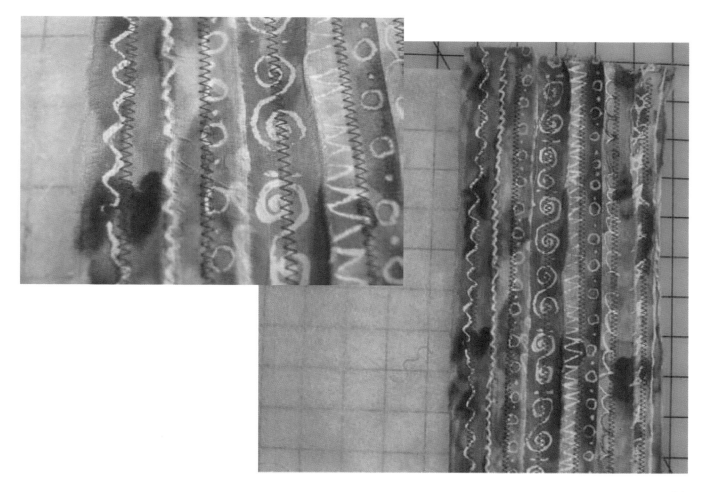

STEP 3: Randomly place the narrow, coordinating fabric strips on the main fabric strips. When you are happy with the placement, stitch these down through the center of the strip with a straight or zigzag stitch.

STEP 4: Cut the fabric strip unit into two pieces that measure 11" x 7". These will be the front and back cover for your book.

STEP 5: Place your book cloth piece on your work surface right side down. Apply glue to one side of the spine piece cut from the book board and center it on the book cloth, glue side down.

STEP 6: Apply glue along the edge of the book cloth keeping it about 1" from the top and bottom edges and place one of the cover pieces cut from the book board on the book cloth.

Place the book board along the glued edge keeping it ¼" from the edge of the spine piece and keeping the top and bottom edges aligned.

Glue the other piece of book board to the other side of the book cloth.

STEP 7: Put some glue along the excess book cloth extending beyond the top and bottom edges of the book and fold these edges over to the inside.

Press them down well to make sure they are attached securely to the book board.

Tip: You can make your own book cloth to match your fabric selections. Simply use a piece of fabric, such as cotton duck shown here, and color it to coordinate. Paint with textile paints, such as Jacquard Dye-Na-Flow, to add vibrant color to the fabric. Allow to dry and heat set with your iron.

STEP 8: Now turn your book over so that the outside is facing you and coat one side of the book board with glue, but do not put any glue on the book cloth.

Take one piece of your fabric strip surface and determine which edge will overlap the book cloth edge. Turn the fabric strip surface over and run a line of glue about ½" wide along the edge on the wrong side. This is the edge that will overlap the book cloth.

Place the fabric strip surface on the book cover where you have applied the glue. Place the fabric on the cover so that the left edge of your strip surface overlaps over the edge of the book cloth by about ¼" and the strip surface extends beyond the top and bottom edges

of the book cover by about 1". There will be more than 1" of strip surface extending beyond the right edge but that's okay, because you'll trim the excess off later.

Press the fabric strip surface down well to be sure that there are no wrinkles or air bubbles and that the strip surface is in good contact with the cover.

Repeat these steps to apply the fabric strip surface to the other side of the book cover.

STEP 9: When you have glued both sides of the cover surfaces on, flip the book over so that the inside is facing up and trim the fabric strip edges to 1". Turn in the corners and glue in place and then fold over the fabric strip edges and glue in place.

STEP 10: Cut a piece of paper measuring 8½" x 13½" to line the inside of your book, and glue it in place.

Set the book aside while you prepare your signatures for the inside.

STEP 11: Prepare five signatures for the inside of your book using paper measuring 8½" x 11" and folded in half to make pages 8½" x 5½".

Using a four-hole punching guide as described in *Making and Sewing Signatures* beginning on page 21, punch the holes in your signatures.

Open up the book cover and with the lining side up, center your hole-punching guide (made with 5 columns of holes for this project) along the center of the spine and mark and punch the holes in the book cover.

Sew the signatures into the book following the four-hole stitching instructions on page 26.

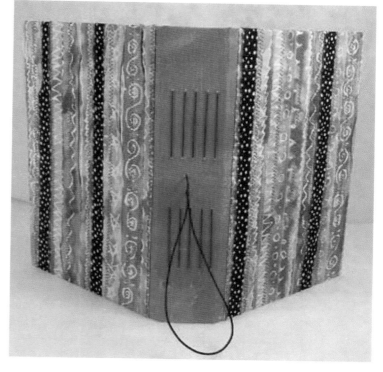

STEP 12: The closure on this book is an elasticized cord with metal ends. This step is optional. To install the cord, punch two holes into the spine between the signatures, trying to center the holes on the spine as much as possible. Punch the holes approximately ¾" apart. From the outside of the book, thread the metal ends of the elastic into the holes you have punched and then bend the ends on the inside so they are flush against the spine. You should have a loop of elastic cord on the outside of your book that you can fold over the front and back cover to hold them closed. If you are using elastic without the metal ends, just tie a knot on the end of your elastic to keep it from slipping through the holes.

Mini Stab Stitched Book

This little book goes together very quickly and is perfect for using up scraps of leftover papers. It makes a nice gift on its own or use leftover wrapping paper and make a book to coordinate with your gift packages at holidays, birthdays or any occasion when you want to add an extra special touch to a gift.

SUPPLIES NEEDED

Book board:
- One piece 5¾" x 3½" (top)
- One piece 3½" x ¾" (top spine)
- One piece 3½" x 6¾" (bottom)

NOTE: The bottom cover of this book has no spine piece; it is just one piece of board.

Wrapping paper to cover the inside and outside covers

Paper for the inside pages of the book cut 6½" x 3½"

STEP 1: Cut a piece of wrapping paper 6" x 9" and glue the cover piece and spine piece to the wrong side aligning the top and bottom edges and leaving a border of 1" all the way around. The spine piece should be ¼" from the cover piece.

STEP 2: Because wrapping paper is relatively thin paper, it's a good idea to add an additional piece of paper over the spine hinge to stabilize it.

STEP 3: Trim the excess paper around the edges to ¾" and fold and glue the excess paper down to the inside.

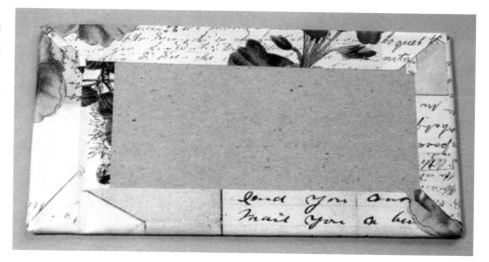

STEP 4: Cut a piece of paper to line the inside of the cover ½" smaller than the size of the cover and glue it in place.

STEP 5: Cover the bottom cover piece (the piece measuring 3½" x 6¾") with wrapping paper the same way omitting a spine piece.

STEP 6: Now it's time to punch the holes. This book has six holes along the edge. Place the holes, evenly spaced, ¼" from the left edge starting ½" from the top and ending ½" from the bottom.

Make the holes in the bottom cover on the left edge with the inside facing up and along the spine edge of the top cover with the inside facing down.

Use the back cover to mark where to punch the holes in your pages.

STEP 7: Now it's time to sew the book together! Place the bottom cover on your work surface inside facing up, place your pages on top and then place the cover on top with the inside facing down.

Thread a tapestry needle with a length of twine or floss that is 24" long.

Follow the photo illustration for the number assigned to each hole along the spine. Refer to these numbers throughout the stitching process. The number I represents the hole closest to the top edge of the book.

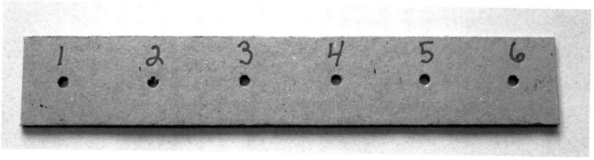

Before you begin sewing decide if you want your finishing knot to appear on the top of the book or on the back side. If you want your knot and thread tails to appear on the cover when you are finished, then begin by passing your needle through hole #4 from the top of the book down through the pages through the bottom cover of the book. If you want it to appear on the back side of the book, then start by passing your needle through hole #4 from the bottom cover of the book through the pages and up through the top cover.

1. Pass the needle through hole #4 through the top cover, the pages and through the bottom cover leaving a 6" tail to be used to tie a knot when you're finished.
2. Pass the needle back around through hole #4 again wrapping the thread around the edge of the spine.
3. Sew through hole #5 from the bottom up through to the top.
4. Sew back around the spine and back up through hole #5 again.
5. Sew down through hole #6.
6. Sew around the right edge of the book and back down through hole #6.
7. Sew up around the spine of the book and back down through hole #6.

8. Sew up through hole #5.
9. Sew down through hole #4.
10. Sew up through hole #3.
11. Sew around the spine back up through hole #3.
12. Sew down through hole #2.
13. Sew around the spine back down through hole #2.
14. Sew up through hole #1.
15. Sew around the top edge of the book and back up through hole #1.
16. Sew around the spine and back up through hole #1.
17. Sew down through hole #2.
18. Sew up through hole #3.
19. Tie a knot with the end you left hanging.

Embellish the thread ends with beads if you like, trim the ends and your book is done.

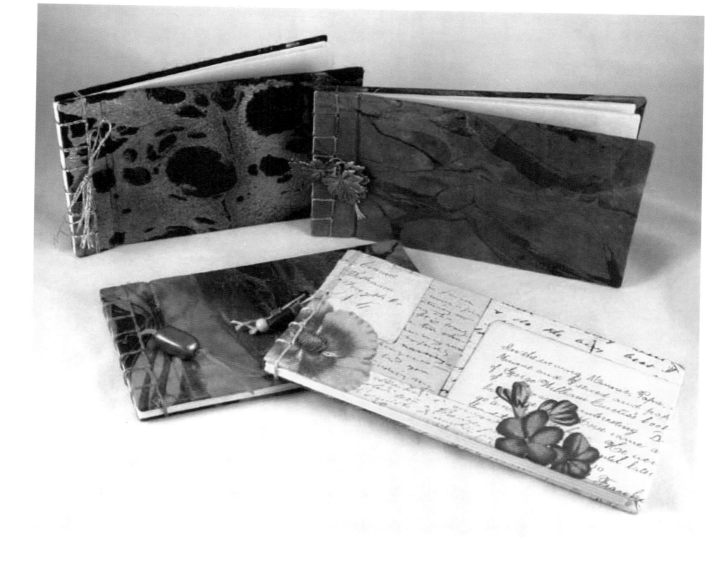

Tip: If you decide to make a larger version of this book you'll want to use more stitching holes to insure that your pages are secure. Consider filling your book with a heavier weight cardstock and using it as a photo album.

Painted Foil Book

In issue five of Fibre&Stitch online magazine, there is an article by Miriam Forder about using kitchen foil as a substrate to cover a book using black ink as the coloring agent. I was intrigued by this technique but wanted to find an alternative to using ink to color the foil. After much experimenting I discovered that using Golden Fluid acrylic paint opens a world of color possibilities and opportunities for layering color over color to create an interesting and dynamic effect on the foil surface.

SUPPLIES NEEDED

Book board:
   Two pieces 9" x 6" (front & back)
   One piece 9" x 1½" (spine)
Book cloth 3" x 11"
Grungeboard or shapes cut from
   cardboard or mat board
PVA glue
Chip brush
Kitchen foil
Golden Fluid acrylic paint
Soft rubber brayer
Stiff stencil brush
Steel wool
Paper to line the inside of the book
Paper for the inside pages of the book

STEP 1: Begin by applying glue to one side of the spine piece and place it on the book cloth centering it both horizontally and vertically.

The book cloth in the example is white, but the color you use isn't important because it will get covered with foil.

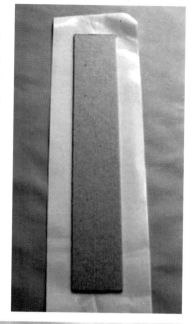

STEP 2: Apply glue along the edge of the book cloth keeping it about 1" from the top and bottom edges and place one of the cover pieces cut from the book board on the book cloth.

Place the book board along the glued edge keeping it ¼" from the edge of the spine piece and keeping the top and bottom edges aligned.

Glue the other piece of book board to the other side of the book cloth.

STEP 3: Put some glue along the excess book cloth extending beyond the top and bottom edges of the book and fold these edges over to the inside.

STEP 4: Turn your book over so that the right side is facing you and glue your shapes to the covers. The piece to the right of the spine will be the cover so keep this in mind when you are gluing your shapes in place.

You can see in the example that several heart-shaped pieces of grungeboard are glued to the covers. You can also use shapes cut from book board, cardboard or even mat board if that's what you have on hand.

STEP 5: Once the pieces have dried in place, tear a piece of foil that's larger than the surface of the book and crumple it lightly. Do this carefully so that you don't tear the foil. Uncrumple it carefully and set it aside.

Coat the entire surface of the book with glue.

Lay your uncrumpled piece of foil on top so that the foil extends beyond all four edges. Use the brayer to press it down onto the surface.

After you have used the brayer, you can use a stiff stencil brush to pounce over the surface and push the foil into the nooks and crevices around the shapes you glued onto the surface.

Tip: Do not cut kitchen foil with your good scissors.

STEP 6: Turn the book over and trim the excess foil along the edges to ½" to 1" depending on how much foil you have to work with.

STEP 7: Apply glue along the excess foil extending over the surface of the book and then turn it to the inside and press it down firmly using the brayer to make sure that it comes in good contact with the book board.

STEP 8: Now it's time to add color! Paint the surface using whatever colors of Golden Fluid acrylic paint that you like. You can use one color or several.

Let the paint dry thoroughly. When it's completely dry you can buff the surface with some fine steel wool. Do this with a light touch because you'll actually be removing some of the paint as you rub across the surface.

Tip: It's a good idea to paint a small amount of the acrylic paint on a scrap piece of foil to make sure that you like the color that you've chosen. Some of the colors look a little bit different on a foil surface than they do on paper.

STEP 9: Cut a piece of paper measuring 8½" x 13½" to line the inside of your book. Glue this piece in place and press the paper down very well to be sure that there are no wrinkles or air bubbles and that the paper is in good contact with the book board.

STEP 10: Prepare three signatures for the inside of your journal using paper measuring 8½" x 11" and folded in half to make pages 8½" x 5½".

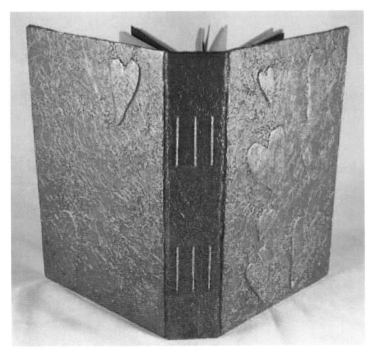

Using a four-hole punching guide as described in *Making and Sewing Signatures* beginning on page 21, punch the holes in your signatures. Open up the book cover and with the lining side up, center your hole-punching guide along the center of the spine and punch the holes in the book cover.

Thread a tapestry needle with an 18" length of embroidery floss, linen twine or other sturdy thread and sew in the signatures following the four-hole stitching pattern on page 26.

TRY THIS:

This book was created by first painting the surface with turquoise and then, when dry, painting over it with copper. When the entire surface was dry it was buffed with a piece of steel wool, which removes a bit of the copper paint and reveals the underlayer of turquoise, creating a wonderful vintage copper look.

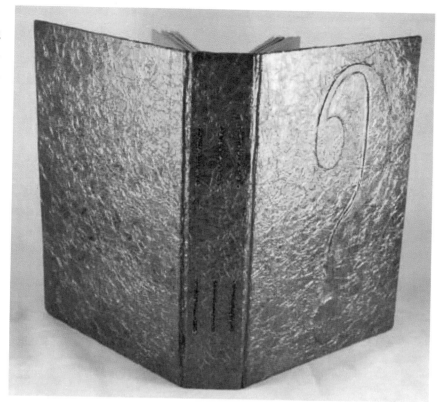

To create these books, two different colors of fluid acrylics were dabbed randomly across the surface. A clean paintbrush was used to blend the colors where they ran together on the surface.

Each one was buffed lightly with a piece of fine steel wool when dry.

CHAPTER 9

Book
Covers

Composition Book Cover

Transform an inexpensive composition book with an artful, custom cover. When you've filled the book just remove it from the cover, slip in a new one and you're ready to start writing again.

SUPPLIES NEEDED

An old pair of jeans
Mistyfuse
Parchment paper
Peltex
Composition book (9¾" x 7½")
Fabric for lining the inside and making
  the sleeves

Everybody has an old pair of jeans in the closet that may have some rips and tears or that don't fit, but you just can't seem to part with. Instead of banishing them to the back of the closet, recycle them into a cover for your composition book.

STEP 1: First you'll need to deconstruct your jeans. Start by carefully removing the back pockets and set them aside.

STEP 2: Turn the jeans inside out and cut off the side seams up to the crotch seam. Cut the top part of the jeans off to separate it from the leg pieces.

Toss the top of the jeans away or save them for another project.

STEP 3: Press the remaining four pieces of jean material well to remove any wrinkles and then cut them into long strips (at least 16½" long) of varying widths from ¾" to 1½".

STEP 4: Cut a piece of Peltex 10¼" x 16" and fuse a layer of Mistyfuse to one side.

Place the strips (right sides up) on top of the Peltex, overlapping each strip so that none of the Peltex surface peeks through.

It's okay to let the strips hang over the edges. You

can trim the excess off after you've fused the strips in place.

When you have all the strips in place, press the surface with a hot iron to fuse them to the Peltex and then trim off any excess from the edges.

STEP 5: Add stitching along the edge of each strip to secure the raw edges in place. You can use a straight, zigzag or other decorative stitch, if your machine has one.

Tip: You can use Jeans thread to stitch the strips in place for a more authentic look. This thread is a heavier weight and has been dyed that special orange/brown color that is used for top stitching on jeans. You'll find it in the fabric store with the other specialty threads usually labeled "Jeans thread".

STEP 6: Fold the book cover in half, wrong sides together, and determine where your pocket will be placed on the front cover.

Open out the cover and sew the pocket in place along the three outer edges using the original stitching lines as your guide.

STEP 7: Turn the Peltex over and fuse a piece of fabric to the other side. This will be the inside lining of your book cover.

STEP 8: To make the inside sleeves that hold the book in place, cut two pieces of fabric 10¼" x 13". Fold these pieces in half, wrong sides together, and press to make two pieces measuring 10¼" x 6½".

Sew the other jeans pocket to one of these pieces. Make sure you place the jeans pocket on the sleeve piece so that the fold is on the left.

STEP 9: Place the fabric sleeves on the lining fabric, one on each end. Align the raw edges of the sleeve with the raw edges of the cover piece. Baste the sleeves in place using a scant ¼" seam allowance.

Zigzag stitch around all four edges of the book cover, slip your composition book inside and you're done!

The composition book cover can be made using most of the surface design techniques shown in this book. Below is another version of the composition book cover. This cover was made with Roc-lon Multi-Purpose Cloth. The cloth was painted with acrylic paints in an allover abstract design. Using marking pens, the text was written and decorated. The cloth was fused to heavy interfacing and constructed as shown in the previous pages.

Tip: Other fabrics could be used in place of the Roc-lon Multi-Purpose Cloth. Cotton duck is one example.

A strip of fabric was fused to the spine area of the cover to add additional visual interest. Zigzag stitching was added along the edges to secure it in place and then free-motion stitching was added over the surface for even more visual and textural impact.

CHAPTER 10

Gallery

Diane Hamburg

Web site: www.dianehamburg.com
Blog: http://dianehamburgart.blogspot.com
Email: dianehamburg@comcast.net

Diane's Thread Doodles and Verses I

Living at the beach, I find much of my inspiration for my fiber art while taking my daily walks by the surf. The sun rising, the gulls flying, the pelicans soaring and diving with thoughts of my loved ones and my life in general thrown in are all inspiration. Haiku poetry fascinates me so I try to form short verses when something catches my attention. I sometimes take a mini sketchbook with me to capture what I see. I arrive back at my home studio and set these words and sketches using thread onto cloth. My self-portrait is "in progress." I had wanted to come up with my own whimsical likeness to use on my art quilt labels.

This fabric book was created using one piece of plain muslin and batting. A fabric rectangle was folded in half lengthwise, opened, turned and folded in half widthwise twice. Using the scissors, I made a cut from the centerfold to the next fold. The rectangle was opened and folded lengthwise again. The ends were pushed towards the middle to make the book shape. I numbered the pages then opened the rectangle again to appliqué and machine stitch. Once I completed the pages, I refolded the book and stitched the edges and the centers, adding fringe to the outside edges.

Photos by Sue Bleiweiss

Lesley Riley

Grow Wings

The book cover is constructed from two 5" x 7" canvas boards that were covered with hand-painted fabric. The title of the book, *Grow Wings*, was transferred directly onto the front cover fabric. On the front cover is a transferred image of a bird, hand stitching and beading embellishments; which were glued on after the construction of the book was complete. Ribbons were inserted between the right sides of the front and back cover and the end papers to create a closure for the book.

Binding detail

A folded length of vintage bark cloth became the spine for the book. To add a bit of further embellishment, a hand-dyed and printed scrap of silk organza was tacked onto the bark cloth. Three signatures of assorted papers were hand stitched through the fabric spine using rayon and cotton ribbons; which were tied on the outside for a decorative finish. Beads were added for further embellishment.

Inside detail

The interior pages of *Grow Wings* are comprised of a variety of papers, some of which vary in size. Left side: Transferred text on unpainted watercolor paper. Right side: Transferred image and text onto resist painted printmaking paper.

Web site: www.LesleyRiley.com

Photos by the artist

Violette Clark

Menopause

Being menopausal some-
times leads to experiencing
hot flashes, memory loss
and a host of other feel-
ings, including depression
and feelings of craziness.
The way I cope with such
things is to create a journal page. Invariably I feel a
sense of peace—journaling
whatever I am experienc-
ing is a cathartic exercise.

Some journaling advice from Violette

Tell your stories only the way YOU can—think of things that happened in your past or today and fashion a journal page
like I have done. Your stories can come alive, be given life and can help you come to terms with events by giving them a
face. It's a very powerful way of moving through your stuff! Of course you can also journal joyful times too—these pages
simply amplify whatever you are experiencing! Have fun with it.

~Violette

Photos by the artist

Why can't you be more like me?

When I was a teenager my sister was embarrassed that I was not more like her—more put together, neater and tidier. My teenage years were not the happiest time of my life. It's taken me many years to accept the way I am. Creating a journal page around these feelings today helps bring some of those melancholic feelings to rest. I now am able to embrace who I am.

Solitude

This journal page emerged from being fed up and totally overwhelmed with people. Shortly after creating this page and noticing that I was almost at the "tipping point", I decided to go away on a short, three-day retreat alone to recharge my batteries. I went to a small island and filled the well up! Isn't it marvelous when our journal pages have poignant messages for us? We simply need to listen to them!

As you can see *Solitude* is a simple page consisting of a face, border and some lettering (with a bit of ephemera thrown in for interest). If you break a journal page down into manageable chunks it's not quite as overwhelming.

Web site: www.violette.ca
Email: violetteclark@shaw.ca

Birds Wing Book

This book was created for my research into living forms during my Art & Design studies for City & Guilds. I chose birds wing patterns as my research project and this was from a stamp sent from Japan which depicted a Japanese pheasant. I found the bird in question and made silk screens of the pattern from the wings. The book was then created as the bird's wing and stamped with the designs on the pages. The book is a concertina style and can expand.

Fossil & Feather Book

For my City & Guilds Diploma in Machine Embroidery, a design brief was required to give purpose to your body of work. This was my design brief for my *Fossil & Feather Book*.

In the fashion industry in the 17th Century, miniature "mock-ups" or "maquettes" of the latest styles were shown to the "Elite" or upper classes in society in order to give a visual and tactile representation of the garments in vogue at the time. These were stitched down to the finest detail using the actual fabrics and embellishments. Including accessories and undergarments. Orders would be procured based on these traveling salesman's samplers. Today with the latest print and computer technology, the visual aspect of fashion and advertising has been captured in great detail: enabling the whole world to see for themselves the latest fashions. However the tactile component is still sadly lacking. A book was created to give a visual and tactile representation of the surface designs and stitch techniques available to the fashion industry on wearables from my design company on corsets and bustiers.

Web site: www.annihunt.com
Email: annihunt@me.com

Photos by Kenji Nagai

Trina Lucido

Color Journal

I love using colored pencils in my art-work and have a few favorite colors that I use over and over. I started saving the "nubs" a few years ago, thinking I'd use them for a special project. One day my little boy was helping sharpen my pencils and put both ends in the sharpener! I liked the idea of having two sharpened ends, so that's when I began to use and collect the "doubled-ended" pencil. I make a lot of handmade books, and one day I got the idea to attach my collection to the cover of a journal. The base of the journal is a hardback Reader's Digest condensed book. I glued the colored pencils to the front and then decided it needed a unifying element, so I applied gesso around the pencils and on the cover. On the back, I created a collage using an old Crayola box and paper wrappers from crayons. What I particularly like about the covers of this journal is that every item that was attached to it; the pencils, brushes and wrappers from the crayons were all tools that I used at one time to create colorful artwork.

The interior pages of the journal are monoprint pages. I colored paper towels with liquid watercolors, then placed a sheet of newsprint over the saturated paper towel and used a rubber brayer to make the print. When the pages were dry, I created three signatures. The spine of the book was prepared by punching holes and setting eyelets. The signatures were stitched into the spine with waxed linen thread; old paintbrushes were used as anchors.

Blog: www.thepaperfleamarket.blogspot.com
Email: thepaperfleamarket@yahoo.com

Photos by Sue Bleiweiss

Angela Grasse

I am solar powered and love beach vacations! Each passing winter in Canada causes me to love the beach even more! If I can't be there in person I can at least dream and create about it.

I created the covers of this journal with painted, stretched artist canvases. The backsides of the canvases act as a shadow box of sorts, which hold my lovingly collected shells. I have attached a small bottle filled with sea glass to the spine. The signatures are made up of plain copy paper as well as pages from an old atlas. I have derived a lot of pleasure incorporating my beach treasures in this journal.

Blog: http://princessbubblescreates.blogspot.com
Email: angela@golden.net

Photos by the artist

I created my fabric book to memorialize my friend Donna who passed away from cancer several years ago. She was special to me and while I was making the book, I fondly recalled the countless hours that we shared creating art together.

The lavishly embellished fabric book measures 7" x 7" and has a total of eight pages. It includes a poem about what cancer can't do, Donna's obituary, her memorial card, copies of actual fabric handkerchiefs and a little photo of her as a small child. The back cover has the words, "Love ya lots!" hand stamped around the edges as well as in the center to remember what Donna always said when finishing a phone conversation.

Tea-dyed muslin fabric was used to construct the pages and each page was heavily embellished with hand beading and embroidery work. French knots and beads were used on the pages to add texture and dimension to the muslin fabric. A computer program was used to add text to the fabric pieces and image transfers were made of the handkerchiefs as well as photos. A rubber stamping alphabet was used on a few pages to add wording. All of the outside edges of the pages are embellished with hanging beads draping down from them. The spine was made from tea-dyed lace that was Donna's and it embellishes the inside and outside edges; evenly spaced eyelets and intertwined organdy ribbon attach and secure the spine together, with the ribbon bow on the cover.

Photos by Sue Bleiweiss

Passages is an artist book I created as a signature piece for an exhibition of quilts and dolls I curated under the same name. The exhibition featured my work and the work of one of my students, Barbara Patterson Mackey. I chose the title *Passages* because the exhibition introduced Barbara's work and allowed me to take my work in other directions. We were both taking a journey, traveling onward. I wrote a poem titled *Passages* and used photo sheets to transfer images of the poem for inside pages and for the doll's face, torso and hands. Other material includes threads, yarns, sequins, beads, ribbon, woven and synthetic fabric. The altered Bendi doll has her hands outstretched, inviting and encouraging others to begin their journey.

Passages
Time gives Passage grace.
Tis lovely, sweet transition.
To march awhile, says Heart,
As befits yon Journey's right.

Tis lovely, sweet transition.
Aromas, cinnamon soft,
As befits yon Journey's right,
To laugh and roll and shout.

Aromas, cinnamon soft,
Touch tender skin and kiss,
To laugh and roll and shout.
Tis Beginning's path, This Passage, Grace.

Web site: www.cathleenbailey.com
Email: mail@cathleenbailey.com

Photos by the artist

Lisa Gallup

This journal began life as a 3" x 5" Moleskine sketchbook. Lisa used bright acrylic paint, self-carved rubber stamps, and rub-on transfers to adorn the cover. The flared, open pages hint at the intense color that this journal holds and begs to be picked up and handled. Lisa's creations are usually very colorful with lots of texture.

Metal embellishments for the spine and index tabs for the pages add texture and excitement to the journal. Fibers from various tags in the journal are peeking out of the top, adding even more interest to the book.

Flickr photos: www.flickr.com/photos/spiritthingstudio
Facebook: www.facebook.com/lisagallup.spiritthingstudio
Email: spiritthing@comcast.net

Photos by the artist

Virginia Spiegel

Lost Garden

This book commemorates a one-third acre landscape that I designed, planted and nurtured for seven years. When I left, the new owners tore out the garden, put the plants in the trash (despite my written plea that they call the local garden club for a plant rescue) and put in grass. This book was started in anger, but became a very calming artwork with the main message to myself being, "Plant again." Aluminum contour mesh, photos printed on silk organza and cotton fabric, hemp cord, marker, ink, hand and machine stitching.

Lost Garden, detail

The main photos of "Lost Garden" are printed on silk organza to symbolize the "ghostly" nature of a garden that has been destroyed. Since the accordion book is built on aluminum contour mesh, it is also translucent when displayed with back lighting.

Web site: www.virginiaspiegel.com
Blog: http://www.virginiaspiegel.com/blog/
Twitter: http://twitter.com/vspiegel

Photos by the artist

About the Authors

Sue Bleiweiss

A self-taught book artist, Sue enjoys spending her days in the studio creating interesting and unique surfaces to make books with. Working with fabric and paper, and usually a combination of both, it's the pursuit of creating something that is a pleasure to touch, as well as look at, that inspires her to continually search for new and unusual techniques to explore. Sue's goal has never been to create a perfect and flawless item. It is to create a piece that excites the viewer's eyes when they look at it, make them wonder when they hold it in their hands and inspire their own imagination when they consider how it was created. Sue teaches several classes in book making through www.twocreativestudios.com. You can learn more about Sue's work and how to purchase it on her web site at www.suebleiweiss.com.

Terri Stegmiller

After a lifetime of experimenting with all types of crafts, Terri began exploring quilting in the early 1990's. She discovered pretty quickly that traditional and bed-sized quilts were not quite her style and began experimenting with mixed media and creating her own designs. Known for her innovative combinations of color and pattern she is inspired by nature, cats and the female face; and enjoys creating artwork that incorporate these elements. When she is not creating art, Terri also enjoys web site design and graphic design work. Terri is the author of *Creative Paper Quilts*, sells her art through her web site at www.terristegmiller.com and teaches online classes through www.twocreativestudios.com.

Resources

Most of the supplies for the projects in this book can be found at your local fabric, craft and art supply stores, but here are some online shopping resources for you:

Paper and book binding supplies

Hollander's
www.hollanders.com
Paper and book binding supplies

The Paper Studio
www.paperstudio.com
Paper and book binding supplies

Volcano Arts
www.volcanoarts.biz
Book binding, soldering, metalsmithing supplies and more

General art, fabric and mixed-media supplies

Blick Art Materials
www.dickblick.com
Art supplies

Fiber and mixed-media art supplies

Dharma Trading
www.dharmatrading.com
Fiber art supplies

eQuilter
www.equilter.com
Fabric & sewing supplies

Friends Fabric Art
www.friendsfabricart.com
Unique supplies for mixed media & quilt art

I Have a Notion
http://ihavea-notion.com/store/
Fiber art supplies

Joggles
www.joggles.com
Everything for the textile, cloth doll & mixed media artist

Long Creek Mills
www.longcreekmills.com
Makers of Stiffy interfacing

Mistyfuse
www.mistyfuse.com
The best fusible web!

Online resources

Two Creative Studios
www.twocreativestudios.com
Take online classes with Sue Bleiweiss and Terri Stegmiller

Fibre&Stitch
www.fibreandstitch.com
Online mixed media fiber arts zine

Further reading

Creative Ways with Fibre&Stitch
By Sue Bleiweiss & Terri Stegmiller
ISBN 978-1440489150

Creative Paper Quilts: Applique, Embellishment, Patchwork, Piecework
By Terri Stegmiller
ISBN 978-1600593123

Cover To Cover: Creative Techniques For Making Beautiful Books, Journals & Albums
By Shereen LaPlantz
ISBN 978-0937274873

Expressive Handmade Books
By Alisa Golden
ISBN 978-1402751813

Unique Handmade Books
By Alisa Golden
ISBN 978-1402706141

Bookworks: Books, Memory and Photo Albums, Journals and Diaries Made by Hand
By Sue Doggett
ISBN 978-0823004911

Bookcraft: Techniques for Binding, Folding, and Decorating to Create Books and More
By Heather Weston
ISBN 978-1592534555

Fabric Art Journals: Making, Sewing, and Embellishing Journals from Cloth and Fibers
By Pam Sussman
ISBN 978-1592531967

Fabric Memory Books: Techniques, Projects, Inspiration
By Lesley Riley
ISBN 978-1600594083

The Art of Fabric Books: Innovative Ways to Use Fabric in Scrapbooks, Altered Books & More
By Jan Bode Smiley
ISBN 978-1571202819

Made in the USA